NORTH EASTERN RAILWAY.

ESHEAD ENGINEER.

SINGLE WHEELER
LOCOMOTIVES

GNR 4-2-2 two-cylinder 8-footer, No. 1007; Stirling's final design. Note the brake pipe on the front buffer beam. These were never installed on his earlier engines as Stirling disapproved of double-heading. Increasing loads, however, eventually made it necessary to fit them. *(NRM)*

The classic lines of GWR 4-2-2 Dean single No. 3031 *Achilles*, built in 1894 and the first of the type to be given a leading bogie from new. Note the GWR coat of arms on the driving wheel splasher. *(NRM)*

SINGLE WHEELER
LOCOMOTIVES

The brief age of perfection 1885 – 1900

Charles Fryer

Oxford Publishing Co.

NER 4-2-2 two-cylinder compound, No. 1517, in superb condition with brasswork gleaming.   (*NRM*)

Dedication

To John and Elizabeth Ransom, Robert and Hughie

A catalogue record for this book is available from the British Library.

ISBN 0-86093-506-X

Oxford Publishing Co. is part of the
Haynes Publishing Group PLC
Sparkford, near Yeovil, Somerset, BA22 7JJ

Haynes Publications Inc.
861 Lawrence Drive, Newbury Park, California 91320, USA

Printed by: BPCC Wheatons
Typeset in Times Roman Medium by BPCC Techset

Contents

MR 4-2-2 Johnson single No. 683 with 7 ft 9 in driving wheels and Deeley smokebox door, at St Pancras. (*Photomatic*)

Introduction

'Many ingenious lovely things are gone', the poet W. B. Yeats lamented sixty years ago. He was not thinking of steam locomotives, but his words will serve as an epitaph on the subject of this book, a late Victorian locomotive type which achieved expression in some of the most handsome engines this country has ever seen, which appear in their day to have run well, sometimes superlatively well, and to have attracted a clientèle of passionate devotees.

These were the inside-cylindered, front-bogie single wheelers, of which eight of the larger independent railway companies had examples built—in one case only a single specimen, in two others as many as 95 and 80 respectively. On one line, the Great Western, they were dignified with names; on the others their artistic lineaments and attractive liveries served to recommend them. All were to some degree the consequence of a rekindled faith in the single wheeler as the best form of traction for fast light trains over moderately graded lines; two won awards at exhibitions, while one set up a speed record which endured for over 27 years.

A chapter has been included on the six 4-2-2-0s which Dugald Drummond built for the London & South Western Railway just before the end of the 19th century. It could be maintained that these were not single drivers at all; it could equally be held that if these are to be included something should also have been said about the Webb three-cylinder compounds, which also had uncoupled driving wheels. However, these latter have had much written about them in praise or derogation, whereas Drummond's half dozen have been largely overlooked. Since each was in effect two single wheelers on one frame, I have included them. I have also refrained

from writing more than a few paragraphs about Patrick Stirling's 8-foot singles on the Great Northern; they preceded the period dealt with, were not inside-cylindered engines and have had a number of books devoted to them.

I have included tables containing the principal details of each of the nine types covered in detail, and wherever possible have given examples of how they performed on the rails, though these descriptions are often necessarily briefer than one would have wished since the recorder noted down fewer details than he might have done. In most cases I have found it fairly easy to obtain good illustrations, but harder in others, often because old glass negatives are now lost or irretrievably damaged. Paradoxically, the type for which I found most pictures was the solitary Caledonian engine. I am specially indebted to the Mitchell Library, Glasgow, for providing some beautiful photographs of this locomotive, and to Mr Nicholson for bringing them to my notice. The National Railway Museum Library in York has also been most helpful in supplying pictures and information. With regard to the two Irish single drivers, I owe Mr R. Clements a special debt of gratitude for some long letters about locomotive running in their time.

If this book and the illustrations in it bring as much pleasure to the reader as researching it has brought to the writer, its production will have been well worth while.

GWR broad gauge 4-2-2 *Iron Duke*, replacing an earlier locomotive of the same name, and generally similar except in being given a cab.　　　　　　　　　　　　　　*(NRM)*

1 The Earlier Generation—1830-1866

From very early years in British railway history it was received orthodoxy that the force exerted by the steam on the pistons in a pair of cylinders should be transmitted through the cranks of an axle to a single pair of driving wheels when fast passenger haulage was intended. This was evident from the time when George Stephenson's *Rocket* first took the rails on the Liverpool & Manchester Railway.

The coupling of axles by a rod on either side in order to augment adhesion had been practised earlier in the same designer's *Locomotion No. 1* of 1825, built for the Stockton & Darlington Railway, but it was regarded as a hindrance to free running, which introduced into the moving parts not merely extra friction in bearings, but also the need to balance the turning and reciprocating masses. Locomotive engineers, proceeding largely by guesswork and rule of thumb, without the benefit of such sophisticated devices as dynamometer cars or stationary locomotive testing plants, assumed these things must be so, and over-estimated their extent. In any case the number of passenger miles travelled daily was a tiny fraction of what it is now, so trains were much shorter and lighter, and adhesion was not the problem that it later became. A few tons' weight on each driving wheel was enough to allow a train of a dozen four-wheeled coaches to be started without slipping if the rails were dry and, if they were wet or greasy, sand dropped in front of the tyres would enable it to get a grip. If, as at Euston in London or Queen Street in Glasgow, a severe gradient began at the platform ends, the locomotive could be helped out by a rope wound around a drum rotated by a stationary steam engine until the top of the incline was reached.

The single wheeler was therefore quite satisfactory as long as loads remained relatively light and the gradients to be surmounted were either of moderate steepness or, if severe, short enough to be climbed without too great a fall in speed. The London & Birmingham Railway may be taken as an example of a good road for such engines. Apart from the rope-assisted 1 in 70 of Camden Bank, the ruling gradient was 1 in 330 until almost within sight of Birmingham station, just before which there were two short steep pitches. Passenger trains as a rule did not much exceed 100 tons and scheduled start-to-stop speeds were never more than in the upper 40s. So on passenger trains, single wheelers of one sort or another were always used, including Alexander Allan's 'Crewe' type of 2-2-2, built first in 1845, Robert Stephenson's 'long boiler' 4-2-0s, Francis Trevithick's almost unbelievable 4-2-2 *Cornwall*, both of 1847 (the latter having its boiler *beneath* the driving axle), Thomas Crampton's monstrous *Liverpool* of 1848 (a 6-2-0 with the driving axle across the footplate behind the firebox), McConnell's 2-2-2 "Bloomers" of the early 1850s, and John Ramsbottom's 2-2-2 'Lady of the Lake' class, graceful engines which, suitably rebuilt, in some cases lasted into the 20th century. Not until Ramsbottom began to construct his 2-4-0 'Newtons' in 1866 was express work on this line,

and the London & North Western Railway which absorbed it, entrusted to engines with four driving wheels.

These two decades saw a gradual smoothing-out and tidying-up in external design and styling. Some of the early locomotives were, to later eyes, comical and uncouth objects. Steam domes might resemble pepper-pots or circular Greek temples in shape. Fireboxes sometimes look to the modern eye like a domestic immersion heater tank. Front buffers, leather-bound over padding, could well have been the bandaged stumps of amputated limbs. Chimneys, built to the upper limit of the loading gauge, could soar to twice as high as the top of the boiler.

But as the years went by the outlandish designs sobered towards a more seemly norm and, from being a mere contraption designed for haulage, the steam locomotive progressed towards the status of a work of art. By the end of the century it was to become at its best the most beautiful object that Victorian engineers could produce. Subsequently, under the constraints of the need to exert more power and of the loading gauge's limitations, a reverse process set in, and engines began to lose their sylph-like appearance, though never quite reaching previous levels of inartistic offensiveness—except perhaps when O. V. S. Bulleid on the Southern Railway produced his famous goods engine of the Q1 class, which many thought must be a sort of practical joke.

By the mid-1860s the dislike of coupling the wheels of passenger locomotives had begun to wear off, and on main lines with heavy gradients Ramsbottom's example began to be followed, 2-4-0s being built. On the Midland Railway the locomotive department at Derby, under Matthew Kirtley, built its last 2-2-2 single wheeler in 1866, and the London & South Western, which beyond Salisbury had some tough inclines, together with the North Eastern which on its main lines had none, followed suit at about the same time. Most other railways, however, went on constructing single wheelers as well as four-coupled types, and a selection of these will now be described.

The main line of the Great Western Railway between Paddington and Newton Abbot was the most easily graded in Great Britain and thus very suited to single wheelers. It had also the advantage of being built to Brunel's broad gauge, with rails slightly more than 7 feet apart, and its loading gauge was correspondingly less restrictive; its locomotives therefore had room to spread themselves and could be made larger than those on other lines. In 1846 Daniel Gooch, the Locomotive Superintendent at Swindon, built *Great Western*, a 2-2-2 with driving wheels 8 feet in diameter, which in the same year ran with a load of 100 tons from Paddington to Exeter, 194 miles, in 208 minutes, taking as little as 78 minutes for the $77\frac{1}{4}$ miles to Swindon; the return journey from Exeter took only three minutes longer. This was performance of a so far unheard-of quality. Unfortunately the engine disgraced itself soon afterwards by breaking

An early Bristol & Exeter Railway broad gauge locomotive, as
rebuilt by the GWR, with 7 ft 6 in wheels and numbered 2008.
(*Photomatic*)

its front axle, and the decision was made, with subsequent similar locomotives, to have an extra pair of
carrying wheels in front. In this engine Gooch dispensed
with a steam dome, employing instead a perforated pipe
along the inside top of the boiler to collect the steam for
the cylinders, and he continued to use this device as long
as he was in charge at Swindon. After building six more
engines generally similar to the prototype, but with
somewhat smaller driving wheels, he launched out on a
sequence of 8-foot 4-2-2s whose special features were as
follows.

The boiler resembled that of *Great Western*, but the
firebox, instead of having a hemispherical top, was
round-topped with its outside cover somewhat raised
above the boiler casing. The outer frames were of the
'sandwich' type, in which a layer of oak was enclosed by
thin steel plating on either side, the axleboxes being
supported within them; in addition, inner plate frames
extended from the cylinders to the front of the firebox.
The driving wheels and rear carrying wheels had external
plate springs, but a single long inverted plate spring on
either side supported at each end the bearing of one of
the front carrying wheels. There was no cab or protective
spectacle plate for the crew.

One of these locomotives, *Lord of the Isles*, was
exhibited at the Great Exhibition, Hyde Park of 1851.
During 1847/51 Swindon built 22 and Rothwell & Co.
a further seven of these engines. After *Great Western* had
been rebuilt with four front carrying wheels the total was
raised to 30 locomotives. The class was so well regarded
that as most of the original locomotives wore out they

were replaced by others similar in almost every respect
except that the boiler pressure was somewhat raised, a
little more weight was put above the driving wheels, and
cabs were fitted over the footplates.

Early in the 1850s the GWR was obliged to adopt a
mixed gauge by laying a third rail on its own routes, so
had to obtain locomotives to suit. Gooch therefore
designed a 2-2-2 type for use with standard gauge
passenger trains, and Beyer, Peacock & Co. of
Manchester built a number. In appearance they resembled the earlier 4-2-2s, but were of course smaller,
and had a driving wheel diameter of only 6 ft 6 in. An
unusual feature of this design was a system of compen-
sating levers between the axles which were intended to
ease out the shocks on the springs and make for a
smoother ride. According to E. L. Ahrons, who did a
great deal of footplate riding in his earlier days, this was
indeed achieved; however, when the time came for
rebuilding, the levers were removed.

For many years the GWR 4-2-2s were the fastest-
running engines in the country. For a while, one train,
regularly hauled by one of them, was timetabled to reach
Swindon from Paddington in 85 minutes with an intermediate halt at Didcot. To achieve this the 53 miles from
Paddington to Didcot would have needed to be run in
well under the hour. Granted, the road was almost level
and lacked any permanent speed restrictions, yet at that
time no other train in the country was booked anything
like as fast as this. There was a rumour that on 11th May
1848 Didcot was reached in $47\frac{1}{2}$ minutes from Paddington. With a light train this was just about possible. It
would have meant long stretches being covered at
70 mph, a speed which would then have seemed almost
dangerously high. If the story is true it probably rep-
resents a record for a locomotive fired by coke, which

Lord of the Isles, 1851 which was exhibited in the Crystal Palace at the Great Exhibition, Hyde Park.   (*NRM*)

was then the only fuel used.

To turn now to the LNWR, unlike the GWR, that company never went in for high speed in its early days but prided itself on timekeeping and reliability. To work express trains on that line's Southern Division it had a number of different kinds of single wheelers built from 1852 onwards, some at Wolverton before the LNWR concentrated its building at Crewe, some at Crewe itself, and some by private firms. Two main designs predominated: the so-called "Bloomers"[1] built by J. E. McConnell when he was Locomotive Superintendent on the Southern Division, whose headquarters were then at Wolverton, and the 'Lady of the Lake' class, built at Crewe by John Ramsbottom. The first "Bloomer" came out in 1851. As originally constructed it carried no driving cab, had inside cylinders and framing, and a built-up dome vaguely suggestive in shape of the Albert Hall (which had not then been built). The driving wheels were 7 feet in diameter. More were built later, some with 7-foot wheels, some with 6 ft 6 in wheels ("Large Bloomers" and "Small Bloomers" respectively), and a little later on a few were turned out with 7 ft 6 in wheels

1. The nickname was not applied when the engines were first built, but many years later, when Mrs Amelia Bloomer, the celebrated pioneer in women's dress reform, went around wearing a sort of feminine equivalent of plus-fours, cheerfully enduring in a good cause the cat-calls and ridicule of those she met in the streets. She showed a lot of leg, the inside-framed engines displayed a lot of wheel—hence the appellation.

for (so it was said) running expresses between London and Birmingham in two hours, which they were never in fact called on to do. Each was unusual in having McConnell's 'Patent Combustion Chamber', an extension of the upper part of the firebox into the boiler barrel, and also in having the cylinders placed so low that they had to be inclined upwards to work the cranks. These, unlike the others, had outside frames. The "Bloomers" were very competent locomotives. In later years, when the LNWR had gone over to the use of four driving wheels on each engine, a "Bloomer" was often used when a 2-4-0 was not available.

Meanwhile, Crewe was building single wheelers, some with 7-foot and some with 6-foot wheels, for use north of that town. There was nothing particularly noteworthy about the earlier ones, but between 1859 and 1865 Ramsbottom constructed a new type of 2-2-2, the 'Lady of the Lake' class. They were outside-cylindered and inside-framed with driving wheels of 7 ft 7½ in in diameter. They were very light engines with short wheelbases. As first built they had no cabs, but when Francis Webb, Ramsbottom's successor, rebuilt them some years later he added cabs, replaced the existing splashers which had radiating oval slots by closed ones, and increased the diameters of their driving wheels to 7 ft 9½ in. In all, 60 were built, and they enjoyed long lives. They were pretty little machines, but their adhesion weight was small, and their short wheelbases made them nose from side to side at speed. Until the advent of Webb's three-cylinder compounds they worked many of the principal expresses

LNWR 2-2-2 'Lady of the Lake' class No. 618 *Princess Alexandra*, as originally built, *circa* 1859, but with cab added.
(Photomatic)

LNWR 2-2-2 'Lady of the Lake' class No. 802 *Red Gauntlet*, as rebuilt with higher-pitched boiler, larger firebox and thicker wheel tyres.
(Photomatic)

south of Crewe. They survived until the turn of the century, and were often used as pilots for the unreliable Webb compounds when loads appeared to call for extra help. The last one was withdrawn in 1906.

Some mention should be made of the rebuilt *Cornwall*, which did not last long in its original form with the boiler slung beneath the driving axle. How it performed in that condition no one knows, but in 1858 Ramsbottom reconstructed it, leaving the outside frames and huge

LNWR 2-2-2 'Lady of the Lake' class No. 184 *Problem*. (*Photomatic*)

No. 184 *Problem* as rebuilt with larger tender. (*Photomatic*)

LNWR 2-2-2 No. 3020 *Cornwall*, with 8 ft 6 in driving wheels—originally built in 1847 with the boiler beneath the driving axle, but reconstructed in 1858 as shown.   (*Photomatic*)

No. 3020 *Cornwall* reflecting the afternoon sunlight at Euston.   (*Photomatic*)

driving wheels, but providing it with a boiler in the more usual place as well as a cab. In effect it now became another 'Lady' with extra-large driving wheels of 8 ft 6 in diameter. No specially rapid running is credited to it; it probably ran quickest when it piloted other engines. Eventually it was relegated to the line between Liverpool and Manchester to work lightly-loaded trains, and it ended its days as the engine attached to the Chief Mechanical Engineer's saloon. It is now preserved at the National Railway Museum, York.

The Midland Railway built its last single wheeler for many years in 1866, the final one of three similar batches whose construction began in 1859. All were designed by Matthew Kirtley. They had inside cylinders, external framing and springing, and no cabs. The first half dozen, built by Robert Stephenson & Co., had the dome on the first ring of the boiler, so close to the chimney as to give the impression that it was trying to shelter behind it. The next batch, built at Derby between 1856 and 1861, had the dome further back on the second ring of the boiler and surmounted by a Salter-type safety valve; the crew also benefited from the addition of a spectacle plate with a bent-back top. Between 1865 and 1866 a further sequence followed, very similar to the second batch. No records appear to have survived of the performance of any of these types.

The Great Northern Railway relied on single wheelers for its chief expresses, almost until the end of the century. Those built after 1866 by Patrick Stirling are

Midland Railway 2-2-2 No. 28, as built by Kirtley in 1865. Note the bell-mouth chimney and primitive form of cab roof.
(*Photomatic*)

described at some length in the following chapter, but the engines of the man whom he succeeded, Archibald Sturrock, are considered here. Sturrock, who had trained as a railway engineer at Swindon under Daniel Gooch, built a number of 2-2-2s in 1860 with driving wheels 7 feet in diameter. In appearance they were reminiscent of the GWR broad gauge 8-footers, having sandwich frames of oak, faced inside and outside with steel plates, and with raised fireboxes. A spectacle plate gave minimal protection to the crew, and every wheel had prominent outside plate springs. He had earlier, in 1853, built a solitary single wheeler with a front bogie, No. 215, similar in design to his later singles but with a longer boiler, inside springing, 7 ft 6 in driving wheels and, of course, the extra front carrying axle. It was the only one he built, since, like *The Great Bear*, Churchward's 4-6-2 of 1908, it proved too large and heavy for the work it had to do.

It possessed one very unusual feature; the sandboxes were placed ahead of the smokebox and dropped their contents in front of the bogie wheels, which was not of much use as a means of securing adhesion since, when the driving wheels reached the point where the sand had fallen, most of it was no longer there, having by then fallen off the rails altogether! Why this engine was built at all is something of a mystery, but at the time that he was appointed, in 1850, Sturrock must have been aware that there was talk of the GNR and North Eastern Railway together running a train between King's Cross and Edinburgh in eight hours, and it is possible that No. 215 was built to show that the GNR could fulfil its part in the undertaking. However, the enterprise never came to pass and the engine remained surplus to the com-

pany's needs, and soon after Patrick Stirling succeeded Sturrock at Doncaster it was withdrawn and scrapped.

The Great Eastern Railway, whose gradients in East Anglia included many short but steep pitches, also built single wheelers for its faster passenger trains. Between 1862 and 1867 Robert Sinclair designed a 2-2-2 of which several were built by three British firms and one French one. Their appearance was unusual. The cylinders were

MR 2-2-2 No. 35, of the same type as No. 28, but rebuilt with a larger boiler, brass safety valve cover and more substantial cab.   (*Photomatic*)

Great Eastern Railway 2-2-2 No. 299, designed by Sinclair, and built by Schneider of Le Creusot, France, as exhibited at the Paris Exhibition, 1867. Note the peculiarly shaped stovepipe chimney and double splashers for driving wheels and cranks.   (*The Engineer*)

PARIS EXHIBITION—LOCOMOTIVE ENGINE FOR THE GREAT EASTERN RAILWAY COMPANY.

CONSTRUCTED BY MESSRS. SCHNEIDER, CREUSOT.

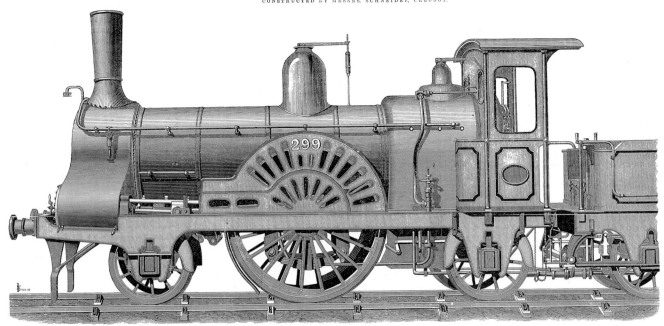

outside the frames but within, not below, the running boards; the stovepipe chimney had a distinct waist, a foot above its point of attachment to the smokebox; the weight taken by the front axle was supported by a single transverse plate spring parallel to it; and both the driving wheel splashers and those of the cranks were embellished by elongated oval radial perforations. The cab was short from front to back but its roof extended well back, and its sides, as also the tender sides, were rather elaborately panelled; there was a touch of the cartoonist Emett about their appearance. They worked on main line expresses for a quarter of a century, but records of how they performed are wanting.

During 1855/6 Joseph Beattie constructed a number of 2-2-2s for service on the London & South Western Railway which had several unusual features. They had outside cylinders, inside frames and (like the GER engines just mentioned) radially slotted driving wheel and crank splashers. There was no cab. The steam dome was a small hemisphere just behind the chimney. Between firebox and boiler a combustion chamber was interposed. Beattie's own special system for pre-heating the feed water featured a vertical condensing tube which projected from the top of the smokebox immediately in front of the chimney. The leading wheels were unusually far back, so that the wheelbase, like that of the LNWR

'Ladies', was very short. A unique feature was a curved pipe which led downwards from the inside base of the smokebox and then curved upwards and forwards to end in a bell-mouth opening. The intention was that when the engine was going forwards at speed, air would be forced into the tube and up into the smokebox to strengthen the draught. The whistle branched out from the front base of the safety valve cover. This type was known as the 'Canute' class, and most of its members were soon reconstructed with coupled wheels. After them the LSWR built no more single wheelers; it was the first company to dispense with them, although, as will be seen later, Dugald Drummond at the end of the century built a few 'double singles' with a 4-2-2-0 wheel arrangement.

The South Eastern Railway built some very handsome single wheelers in 1863 to work its Continental boat trains. They looked very like Kirtley's singles on the Midland, being 2-2-2s, with double frames, outside plate springs and inside cylinders, and safety valves both on the tops of their domes and above their fireboxes. They had no easy task on the line to Folkestone and Dover

The SER 2-2-2 designed by Cudworth, as first built in 1861. Note the length of the firebox and the absence as yet of side sheets to the spectacle plate. (*The Engineer*)

EXPRESS PASSENGER LOCOMOTIVE, SOUTH-EASTERN RAILWAY.

DESIGNED BY MR. J. I'ANSON CUDWORTH, LOCOMOTIVE ENGINEER, ASHFORD.

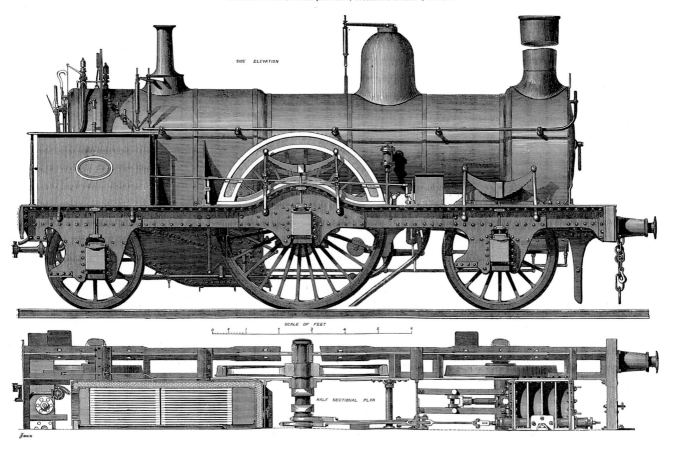

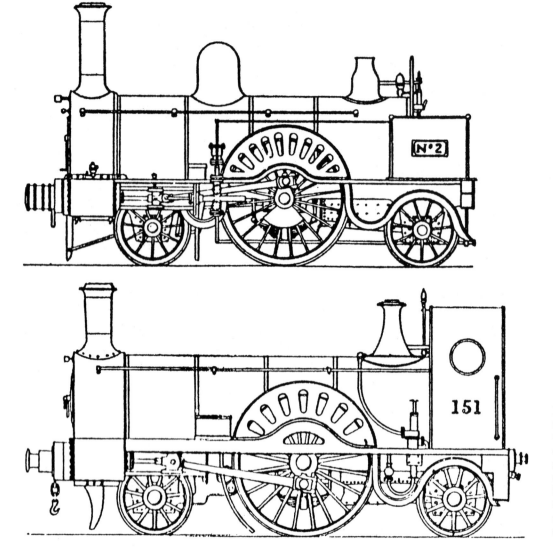

Line drawing of Patrick Stirling's first 2-2-2 for the Glasgow & South Western Railway. Note the primitive buffers, rim-splashers over the leading and trailing wheels and the unusual position of the counter-balance weight on the driving wheel.

Line drawing of Stirling's final 2-2-2 for the G&SWR. Note the domeless boiler and its conical brass safety valve cover, characterizing all his subsequent designs; also the 'porthole' cab, repeated in his first GNR design.

along a road whose gradients in places were quite steep. Loads were usually about 140 tons. However, they did their work successfully and were used on the best trains for a quarter of a century. They were the last single wheelers to be built for the SER.

Going now north of the Border: Patrick Stirling, appointed in 1853 as Locomotive Superintendent of the Glasgow & South Western Railway at the early age of 33, built three types of 2-2-2 in succession for passenger work, and it is interesting to see in them how his ideas developed towards his crowning achievement on the GNR. In 1857 he built his first single wheeler of the 2 class, of which by 1860 there were 13. This type had outside cylinders, a domed boiler, 6 ft 6 in driving wheels, a short wheelbase and an adhesion weight of 11 tons. Curving splashers over the rims of the rear carrying wheels each descended in an S-shaped curve from the rear of the driving wheel splasher. There was no cab. These locomotives were set to work on the principal trains between Glasgow and Carlisle by way of Dumfries, which as a rule were lightly loaded.

In 1860 Stirling brought out another design of 2-2-2, the 40 class, of which ten appeared by 1864. Similarly dimensioned to the 2 class, and similar in appearance below the boiler, this type differed in having no dome; instead, a perforated pipe along the inner top of the boiler served to collect the steam for the cylinders. This feature was to characterise all Patrick Stirling's subsequent designs. A cab was also provided—or perhaps one should term it a canopy, since it had no sides, only a roof. The spring-balance safety valve under the polished brass casing also became an unalterable feature of all his subsequent engines.

In 1865, just before he left Kilmarnock for Doncaster, Stirling produced his third type of single wheeler, the 2-2-2 45 class, which continued to be built after he had gone south. The typical Stirling cab, having a short flat roof with rounded edges, now appeared for the first time, this particular version having side portholes. The size of the driving wheels increased to 7 feet and the wheelbase was also a little longer. If one mentally replaces the front pair of carrying wheels with an imaginary bogie, one can

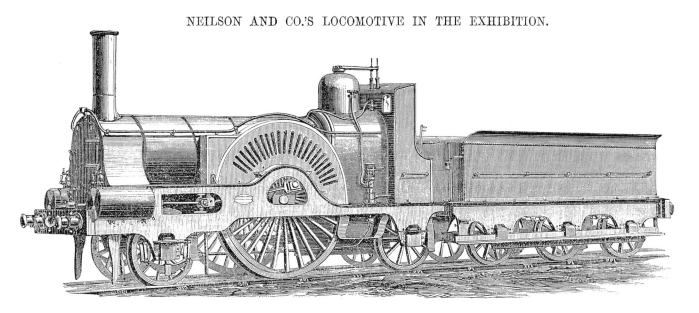

NEILSON AND CO.'S LOCOMOTIVE IN THE EXHIBITION.

Caledonian Railway 2-2-2, designed by Conner with 8 ft 2 in driving wheels, as first built with the dome above the firebox and a primitive cab.   (*The Engineer*)

CR 2-2-2 No. 87, as shown in the previous illustration, but rebuilt with the dome above the boiler and a more effective cab. Note the huge brake-blocks and the bell on the tender to warn the driver of the need for an emergency stop, with the loop of cord for attachment to the train.   (*NRM*)

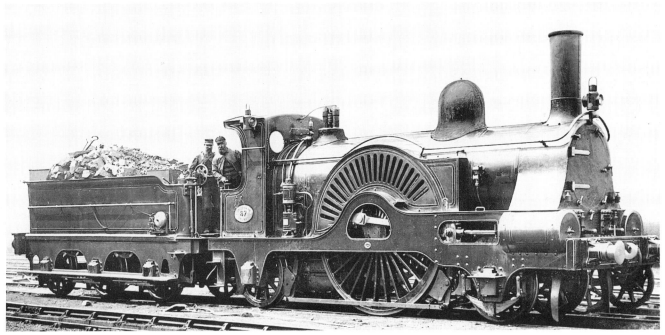

now almost see the later Great Northern 8-footer. These engines replaced their predecessors on the principal expresses before being ousted in their turn by the coupled locomotives built by James Stirling, Patrick's brother, who succeeded him at Kilmarnock.

Finally, mention must be made of the twelve single wheelers built by Benjamin Conner for the Caledonian Railway between 1859 and 1865. These had outside cylinders and driving wheels which out-Gooched Daniel

Gooch's 8-foot wheels on the GWR, being 8 ft 2 in across—astonishing when one thinks of the long gradients on the CR, pitched between 1 in 75 and 1 in 100. They had adequate cabs, which was important north of the Border where the weather can be inclement at all seasons, and as much as $14\frac{1}{2}$ tons of adhesion weight. As first built their domes surmounted their fireboxes, but these were moved later to the second ring of the boiler barrel. Their enormous driving wheel splashers each had

24 radial slots, and immediately around the centre of each driving wheel the running plate came out laterally to form a second splasher which covered the crank and connecting rod big-end. The frames were double and the smokebox sides curved out to meet the tops of the cylinder covers in a manner similar to that of Patrick Stirling's later 8-footers on the GNR. The driving wheels were of steel, unusual at that time, and frequently broke in service. Their chimneys were stovepipes, tall and inelegant. They worked the express trains between Carlisle and the two Scottish capitals for many years before Dugald Drummond replaced them with his 66 class 4-4-0s during 1883/4. No records exist of how they performed.

* * *

The first thing that has to be admitted, when one looks for authentic accounts of how well these earlier single wheelers coped with the trains entrusted to them, is that there are very few of them and that the records which do survive are scanty in detail. The practice of timing express trains, later the hobby of many railway enthusiasts, was then carried on by only a few, and what was done was only very sketchy. The best places from which to obtain information are E. L. Ahrons' book *The British Steam Railway Locomotive: 1825–1925* and his sequence of articles entitled *Locomotive and Train Working in the latter part of the Nineteenth Century*, published in the *The Railway Magazine* between 1915 and 1927 and later republished in six volumes under the same title (edited by L. L. Asher, Heffer, Cambridge, 1951–4). Fortunately a number of these engines survived long enough to be timed by Charles Rous-Marten and some of his contemporaries, though often they had then been rebuilt from their original state, and were performing as well or better than they had done in their youth.

In considering the evidence that *does* exist about early performances, it needs to be borne in mind that both the locomotives and the rails they ran upon were not built of the same kind of hard and tough steel as became available later when better methods of manufacture had developed. Boilers could not be pressed much beyond 120 lbs per square inch. Wheel tyres wore more readily and (a more serious matter) more unevenly. Wrought iron rails had less elasticity than steel ones. So the speeds that were run later, averaging 50 mph or so with maxima of 70 or more, could not then be safely attempted. One does not therefore have to assume that many splendid racing performances went unrecorded. The probability is that there were almost none.

For a good many years the GWR led in the matter of speed. It had the advantage of a very level line—the only main line out of London which did not have to surmount any ranges of hills since it followed the valley of the Thames. It has already been mentioned that some very fast running was performed on special occasions, but not until about 1880 do authentic records begin to emerge, and by then the GWR was not what it had been. The

fastest trains then and for many years before had been available only for those travelling 1st or 2nd class. The two most celebrated expresses were the "Flying Dutchman" and the "Zulu" (nicknames which bore no relationship to their destinations—the first left Paddington for Penzance a little before mid-day, while the second departed for Plymouth in the middle of the afternoon). For many years both were booked to reach Swindon, $77\frac{1}{4}$ miles, in 87 minutes, but (according to E. L. Ahrons) there seems to have been a tacit understanding between the drivers and their engines that it was not necessary to keep so fast a schedule, which was regularly honoured in the breach rather than the observance, with a few minutes being lost to Swindon and regained on the more slowly timed subsequent stretch to Bath.

Ahrons mentions a run behind the 4-2-2 *Rover* on which no higher speed was attained than 58.1 mph between Paddington and Swindon, reached four minutes late; on other occasions 60 mph was reached but time was still lost. Onwards to Bath $66\frac{1}{2}$ mph was the highest rate he ever noted. In the opposite direction, between Swindon and London, where the very slight gradients were in the engine's favour, with the same 87-minute timing a couple of minutes might be gained. Not until the days when the line had been converted from broad to standard gauge did the GWR recover its reputation for speed; during the 1870s and 1880s it had lost it to the GNR. Ahrons, however, on another part of the line did once clock a personal record. He was on the footplate of the 4-2-2 *Lightning* which with a load of about 125 tons passed the 80 mark on the 'up' "Zulu" descending from Whiteball Summit to Taunton.

Some records exist of the doings of the "Bloomer" and 'Lady of the Lake' singles on the LNWR, but only after they had been rebuilt from their original conditions by Francis Webb, and given new boilers and cabs. Ahrons timed two runs in 1877 and 1878, with a 7 ft 6 in and 7 ft "Bloomer" respectively, between Nuneaton and Willesden Junction, when the $91\frac{3}{4}$ miles were covered by the first engine, *Caithness*, in 112 minutes, and by the second, with a slightly heavier load, in $115\frac{1}{4}$ minutes. It is just possible that the mile-a-minute rate was reached on the first run. On both occasions time was kept. In judging these performances one has to remember that the boiler pressures had been reduced on rebuilding to only 120 lbs per square inch. On another occasion Ahrons recorded a time of $93\frac{3}{4}$ minutes between Willesden and Rugby with a 120-ton load by a 7-foot "Bloomer", when the stretch between Bletchley and Wolverton was covered at just over 60 mph. About these locomotives he remarks:

"The "Bloomers" were excellent engines, considering their small tractive power, and the secret of their phenomenal performances probably lay in the free exhaust. The Crewe authorities of that period were said not to have been particularly fond of them. The large engines ... with 7 ft 6 in wheels were relegated to secondary work whenever possible, though their services had to be requisitioned at

Early GWR 4-2-2 non-bogie broad gauge locomotive *Lightning*, of the 'Iron Duke' class (built 1847/51). E. L. Ahrons recorded a maximum of 81 mph with this engine on the descent from Whiteball to Taunton with a 125-ton load.
(*Photomatic*)

times on the best trains. The main line drivers used to say that Crewe was afraid of them."

They were, of course, not products of Crewe but of Wolverton.

The 'Lady of the Lake' class were by the later 1870s too light to be used on any but selected trains. Records of their running at this time do exist; they were largely being used on the light and somewhat easily timed Irish Mail trains to and from Holyhead. Ahrons recorded some performances on the Crewe–Stockport section with moderate loads; typically they covered this more or less level stretch of $25\frac{1}{4}$ miles in from 30 to 35 minutes, and on no occasion did the speed reach 65 mph. However, when put to it a 'Lady' could perform very respectably. This type was used on the four-coach Edinburgh train between Euston and Crewe, $158\frac{1}{4}$ miles, during the 1888 'Race to Edinburgh'. On these occasions they showed that they had a potential for running fast. The best run was made in 178 minutes with three intermediate checks, the net running time being some ten minutes less. Between Nuneaton and Lichfield the average speed was not much under 70 mph, and that speed must have been exceeded at one point at least. This was very fast running for the usually sedate LNWR.

Ahrons also noted some records of running by Sinclair's 2-2-2s on the GER and expressed the opinion that they did "wonderfully good work in their day . . .

at one time they were amongst the first rank of celebrated express engines." He recorded an early run between Ely and Trowse (just short of Norwich) with No. 288, when the $52\frac{3}{4}$ miles were covered in $68\frac{3}{4}$ minutes with a nine-coach load (perhaps 120 tons), the unrebuilt engine having a boiler pressure of only 120 lbs per square inch, and the train not being continuously braked. Later, in 1879, the rebuilt No. 277 made the same run in $3\frac{1}{4}$ minutes less, with four more coaches. Rous-Marten timed a run between Spalding and Lincoln, $38\frac{1}{4}$ miles, with a seven-coach load behind one of these locomotives, when it took only 40 minutes; once it had gathered speed it maintained from 60 to 65 mph the whole way, on level track, and so made up seven minutes of a late start. For the usually leisurely GER this was phenomenal running. Perhaps a special effort was being made to please the observer.

On the South Eastern Railway the best trains were the so-called "Tidals", boat trains whose departures from London and arrivals at the Channel ports were adjusted to the times of high water at the harbours. For a long while these were worked by the 7-foot singles mentioned above, and by 1880 these were getting pretty old. Some of these trains were booked to cover the $26\frac{1}{2}$ miles between Tonbridge and Ashford in 28 or 29 minutes, over a road which, although almost dead straight, is by no means level; there is a 4-mile climb from Headcorn to Chart up gradients which culminate in over half a mile at 1 in 220. On the morning mail train from Cannon Street to Folkestone, Ahrons, in a 15-coach train headed by No. 204, noted a time of 74 minutes from the start to passing Ashford, where two coaches, in one of which he was travelling, were slipped. The distance is $54\frac{1}{2}$ miles and slow running was necessary for some distance beyond the London terminus; there were then steep gradients as far as Knockholt Summit, another minor summit at Sevenoaks, a slack to 30 mph through Tonbridge and the rise to Chart already referred to. This was excellent work by an old engine which by that time was almost due for the scrap heap.

Runs such as these give some indication of what these older single wheelers could do. Their performances no doubt look mediocre when contrasted with the efforts of their successors built during the period next to be considered; these, running on better track and themselves made of better materials, could be much more sprightly, as will be seen.

South Eastern Railway 2-2-2 No. 72, designed by Cudworth for working the 'Tidal' boat trains. Note the embryonic cab—spectacle plate, partly side-sheeted, but without roof.   (*NRM*)

2 The Middle Generation—1867-1884

Patrick Stirling, who replaced Archibald Sturrock as Locomotive Superintendent on the Great Northern Railway in 1866, believed as firmly in the single wheeler as the most desirable type of express passenger locomotive as his father, the Reverend Robert Stirling of Kilmarnock, had believed in the Westminster Confession, and in that faith he lived and died, his last and largest 8-foot single wheelers emerging from Doncaster as he was breathing his last. More than in the case of any other locomotive engineer, his name has been associated with one particular design, the domeless outside-cylindered single with driving wheels of 8 ft 1 in diameter, which became so famous as to be pictured on a South American postage stamp. One of these locomotives has been preserved at the National Railway Museum, York. These engines have probably had more print devoted to them than any other type of Victorian locomotive, but we cannot pass them by here with a mere mention, though they were not quite of the same type as the ones which this book is chiefly concerned to describe.

Stirling has had his detractors as well as his admirers. He was obviously mistaken in his supposition that a coupled engine could not run as freely as a single wheeler. The GWR's *City of Truro* proved that in 1904, and in 1938 *Mallard* rammed the fact home. It is also questionable whether he was right in his contention that the larger the diameter of the driving wheel, the better it would grip the rail for any given weight upon the axle; this has never been shown to be the case. In theory a circular wheel tyre should depress very slightly the rail it rests on, so that it makes contact not at a point but over a very small area, which latter would be greater if the wheel's radius were larger. So a large driving wheel should slip less readily than a small one. This, however, has never been demonstrated in practice.

However, Stirling served his company well during his lifetime. He was expected to provide locomotives that would run fast and reliably with trains of 200 tons and under, and while he lived his single wheelers did that with a minimum of fuss and need of attention. One might contrast him with O. V. S. Bulleid, the Southern Railway's last Chief Mechanical Engineer, who also built famous and eye-catching locomotives which could perform astonishing feats, but which also spent far too much time in the repair shops. Stirling was well liked by his enginemen, who understood the art of managing his single wheelers. One of the surprising things about them was their ability to climb inclines. No very high downhill speed was ever recorded of an 8-footer—his later 2-2-2s could beat them in that respect, despite their smaller driving wheels—but as some of the records indicate, they could surmount the summit at Potters Bar, 12.7 miles from King's Cross, in under 20 minutes with quite substantial loads. Charles Rous-Marten once timed one to cover the distance in 19 min 58 sec with a load of 246 tons, and during the 1895 'Race to Aberdeen' No. 668, with 101 tons, managed on one occasion to do it in 15 minutes. (On this occasion the recorder seems to have been timing to the nearest half-minute, but even if one allows that $15\frac{1}{4}$ minutes might have been the correct timing, that indicates a speed of fractionally under 50 mph, start to pass, with $1\frac{1}{4}$ miles at 1 in 107 and 8 miles at 1 in 200 to be climbed—an astonishing feat.)

Stirling designed his first single wheeler as soon as he arrived at Doncaster, the prototype appearing in 1868 and a further twelve by the end of 1870. Unlike the engines he built for the G&SWR, these had inside cylinders and outside bearings for the carrying wheels. The driving wheels were all 7 ft 1 in across except in the case of the last engine, in which he re-used the 7 ft 6 in wheels of Sturrock's 4-2-2 when the latter was withdrawn. The wheelbase was longer than in any of his Scottish engines—as much as 17 ft 6 in for the last of the batch. The boiler was of course domeless, with a perforated pipe, and the cab was similar to that used on his 45 class G&SWR engines, with a circular window in each side. All the wheels had interior plate springs, and the driving wheels had radially slotted splashers according to the prevailing fashion. To these engines he added rebuilds of six 2-4-0s which Sturrock had built in 1866, turning them into 2-2-2s of about the same size and dimensions as his own, though retaining Sturrock's outside sandwich frames and external springing. He also gave them cabs of the new cut-away type without portholes, with which he had already begun to equip his 8-footers.

These two locomotive types proved satisfactory enough in practice, except in being a trifle unsteady at speed. When the opening of the direct line between Doncaster and York by way of Selby became imminent, and accelerations of the trains from King's Cross to Scotland were being proposed, Stirling decided that more powerful engines would be needed, and that these would have to be steadier at speed. A type with a leading bogie seemed to be indicated. Not many such engines had been built at that time for British lines, and there was no need specially to consider a type which would readily negotiate curves, as the GNR had an unusually straight main line.

Stirling was no champion of bogie engines as such; of all the locomotives which he built during his 29 years at Doncaster, it was only his 8-footers which were so fitted. However, the exigencies of design pushed him in that direction. Once he had decided on very large driving wheels, that meant he could not use interior cranks on their axle unless the boiler were to be pitched much higher than was then considered safe. So there had to be outside cranks, and therefore outside cylinders. The only way to arrange these, if the wheelbase was neither to be inordinately short or long, was to support the leading end of the locomotive on a four-wheeled bogie whose wheels at either side came before and behind the cylinders.

Unhampered now by the need to have cranks beneath the boiler, Stirling made another departure from standard practice and lengthened the cylinder stroke to 28

Great Northern Railway 2-2-2 designed by Stirling in 1868. Note the general similarity to his last G&SWR design, apart from inside cylinders and outside frames.   (*NRM*)

GNR No. 776, 4-2-2 Stirling single wheeler of 1870 with 8-foot driving wheels. Note the absence of a front brake pipe and the presence of a lamp bracket on the chimney.

inches, an unprecedented figure in a British express locomotive. This increased the force exerted by each piston thrust and slightly improved the leverage on the cranks. The driving wheels in the earliest-built 8-footers had plate springs beneath the axle; later-built ones were given a pair of coil springs under the bearings instead. The bogie wheels had a continuous curved channel splasher over their upper rims on either side; the rear carrying wheels had no splashers. Internal plate springs supported all six carrying wheels. The bogie pivoted on a pin 3 inches behind its midway line. Only a small part of the weight of the engine's front end was borne by the pivot; the rest was supported by two side bearings, each one a channel-shaped bracket enclosing one side of the bogie frame, and a slight amount of lateral movement was allowed here.

The boiler was exactly 4 feet in diameter, so that there was only just enough room on either side between its outer covering and the flange of the driving wheel. The firebox in each of the first twelve locomotives had, when first built, a hollow transverse inclined mid-feather made of copper, containing water continuous with that in the boiler, instead of the usual brick arch. The intention was to increase the firebox heating surface at the place of greatest heat, but the device does not seem to have given satisfaction, and in later 8-footers it was discarded in favour of a brick arch, the older engines being reconstructed to match when they came in for heavy repair.

The most striking feature of this locomotive type was the way in which the running plates arched above the cranks on either side, Stirling not wishing to cover the latter with a valance of any kind. This made it easier for the driver to perform his task when he made his rounds with the oil-can, and also provided a feast for the eyes of any observer who saw one of these engines approach-

ing at speed; in the words of R. T. C. Holt, "the 8-footer displayed a heart-stopping poetry of motion as gleaming connecting rods grasped and swung the mighty wheels."

The cut-away cab was a simpler version of the earlier porthole cab. The side windows were no longer provided; the curved edges to the top remained but the sides were less wide from front to rear from waist-height upwards. The chimney was at first of the customary built-up type, but later 8-footers were fitted with a plain one-piece cast iron chimney which tapered out slightly from base to top. A conical brass cover concealed the Ramsbottom safety valve whose lever protruded backwards through a hole into the top of the cab.

A peculiar and apparently retrograde feature in this design was the smallness of the grate area; this meant that more coal would have to be burned in any given time when the engine was in motion in order to raise enough steam. Even here, however, Stirling was the canny Scot. His answer to his critics was that all locomotives had perforce to spend most of their time stationary between duties, and *then* the smaller grate consumed less coal. He also kept the grate area down because he wished to have as wide a water-space around the sides of the firebox as possible, to improve the circulation of water in the boiler.

An observant bystander, looking at the front end of an 8-footer in Stirling's day, would have seen that something appeared to be missing—a brake-connecting pipe on the buffer beam. This reflected a deliberate policy. Stirling refused to countenance double-heading on any fast train, and during most of his lifetime the weights of GNR expresses were sufficiently light to enable timekeeping without resource to piloting. At the end of the century, however, loads began to increase as heavier passenger vehicles were used, and eventually he

The right-hand driving wheel of a Stirling 4-2-2 8-footer, No. 1. (*Photomatic*)

GNR 4-2-2 Stirling 8-footer No. 547 on a 'down' express at Finsbury Park, June 1899.   (*Ken Nunn Collection, LCGB*)

GNR 4-2-2 Stirling 8-footer No. 544, as rebuilt by Ivatt with a domed boiler, at Peterborough in March 1903.

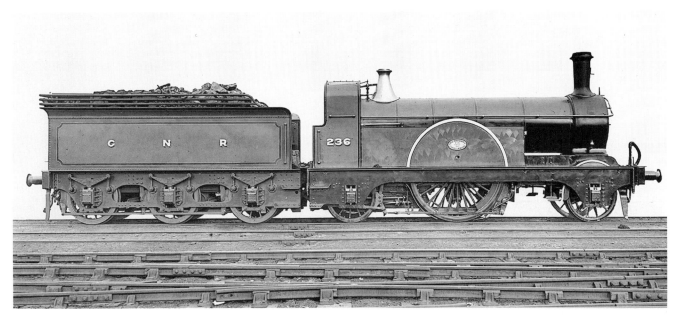

GNR 2-2-2 Stirling 7 ft 7 in single No. 236, as originally built
in 1885.   (*NRM*)

was obliged to reverse his decision and have front brake
pipes fitted to all his locomotives.

The 8-footers were built in yearly batches of two, so
that it took some time for a stock to be built up. They
worked between King's Cross and York, with changing
points at Peterborough, Grantham and Doncaster, some
being shedded at each of these five places. For a while
he relied on them alone for hauling the best GNR

expresses. In 1885, however, he began to build inside-
cylindered 2-2-2s again, similar in general design to the
ones he had constructed in 1868 but with somewhat
larger cylinders, driving wheels of 7 ft $7\frac{1}{2}$ in diameter, and
a long wheelbase of 19 feet, slight lateral play being
allowed to the front carrying wheels. Boilers, fireboxes
and cabs were similar to those of the 8-footers. In fact,
the newer type of engine was slightly the more powerful

GNR 2-2-2 Stirling 7 ft 7 in single No. 235, as rebuilt by Ivatt,
seen at Peterborough, March 1903.

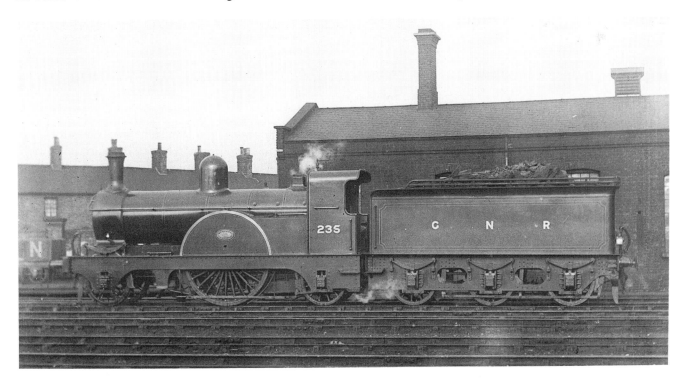

of the two, and in practice performed just as well, higher maximum speeds being recorded of them than of the 8-footers. In all, 26 were built between 1885 and 1894.

Although it takes the story of the GNR 8-footers rather beyond the period covered in this chapter, it seems best to continue it by saying something about the final batch of six which came out in 1894/5. Their construction was perhaps a last-minute attempt to prove that the design was still up to requirements. Stirling now increased the sizes of the cylinders and firebox, and somewhat enlarged the grate area, while at the same time slightly lessening the total heating surface. Externally they could be distinguished by their closed driving wheel splashers and by the fact that their cab tops were extended slightly backwards. As built and first used they had a higher adhesion weight than the rest, carrying (according to official figures) $19\frac{1}{4}$ tons on their driving wheels (in fact it was probably almost 20 tons). How much better they might have been than their smaller sisters was never really shown, for Stirling died as they began to emerge from Doncaster and his successor had other ideas about how to cope with increasing train loads. Furthermore, two serious accidents occurred in which this type was involved, and in the enquiry conducted into one of them excessive weight on the driving wheels was held to be a contributory factor. Stirling's successor, therefore, H. A. Ivatt, had the springing altered to lower the adhesion to 18 tons, after which there was little difference between them and the earlier 8-footers.

GNR 4-2-2 Stirling 8-footer No. 1006, of his final design, with larger cylinders and a backward extension to the cab roof, at Peterborough in July 1904.   (*Ken Nunn Collection, LCGB*)

Ivatt also rebuilt many of the 4-2-2s and 2-2-2s after he had succeeded Stirling, giving them new boilers with domes, after which they performed as well as could be expected, but somehow they did not look right.

To turn now to the Great Western Railway, this company, like the GNR, continued to build single wheelers for its chief passenger trains right up to the last decade of the century. The process culminated, as will be seen in a later chapter, in the construction of bogie 4-2-2s by that wayward genius, William Dean, which were even more noted for brilliant performance than Stirling's 8-footers. Until 1892 the GWR was partly a broad gauge and partly a standard gauge railway, much of it being laid to both gauges by the addition of a third rail. Over the broad gauge to Penzance by way of Bristol, Exeter and Plymouth, the 4-2-2s first built by Gooch prevailed, new ones of similar design replacing the older ones as the latter wore out. Over the rest of the system north and west of Oxford, which had been laid to the standard gauge from the beginning, engines built at Wolverhampton had been used, and the man who succeeded Gooch as Locomotive Superintendent at Swindon in 1864, Joseph Armstrong, had previously been in charge at Wolverhampton and built locomotives there. So far he had constructed no single wheelers but, once established at Swindon, he began to prepare designs for such engines

GNR 4-2-2 Stirling 8-footer No. 93, as rebuilt by Ivatt, at King's Cross in August 1905.   (*Ken Nunn Collection, LCGB*)

GNR 2-2-2 Stirling 7 ft 7 in single No. 233, as rebuilt by Ivatt with a domed boiler and extended cab roof, at York in June 1900.
(*Ken Nunn Collection, LCGB*)

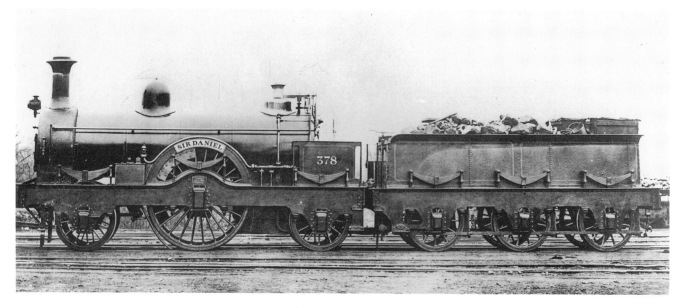

GWR standard gauge 2-2-2 No. 378 *Sir Daniel*, as first
constructed without a roofed cab.   (*Photomatic*)

for standard gauge service between London and places
beyond Oxford, leaving his son, George Armstrong, to
build locomotives for local work at Wolverhampton,
most of these being tank engines.

During 1866/9 he produced 30 2-2-2s with outside
frames and inside cylinders which, after the name given
to the first, were collectively known as the 'Sir Daniel'
class. Each was notable for having what was for the time
a large boiler, 2 inches wider than those of Stirling's
8-footers, and a large heating surface. There was no cab
and every wheel had prominent outside plate springs.
Nothing is known of how they performed in their
original state, and two-thirds of them were to suffer the

unusual fate of being converted into 0-6-0s at the end of
the century; in this rebuilt condition one survived until
1920. Those not rebuilt were modified by Armstrong's
successor, Dean, and joined the batch next to be described in working expresses from Paddington on the
Wolverhampton road. Charles Rous-Marten recorded a
notable performance by a rebuilt 'Sir Daniel' in an
article in *The Engineer* in 1898, described in the latter
part of this chapter.

During 1873/5 Armstrong constructed a further 21
2-2-2s of the 'Queen' class. *Queen*, the first to be built,
which for a long time was used to haul Royal Trains, had
a domed boiler and generally resembled the 'Sir Daniels'

GWR standard gauge 2-2-2 No. 478 of the 'Sir Daniel' class,
un-named, as rebuilt.   (*Photomatic*)

GWR 2-2-2 No. 378 *Sir Daniel*, as rebuilt, heading the 'up' "Northern Zulu" near Shrewsbury in June 1893.
(*P. W. Pilcher Collection, NRM*)

but was a little larger, with a longer wheelbase, cylinders an inch wider, a slightly larger boiler, a slightly increased grate area and heating surface, and a water-filled mid-feather in the firebox. The latter, like the similar device tried out by Stirling, proved unserviceable and was later removed. The other 20 were like the prototype except in having domeless boilers with perforated pipes. Dean later rebuilt them all with domed boilers and cabs and removed the mid-feathers, replacing them with brick arches, at the same time slightly increasing the grate area. As reconstructed they worked with success alongside the 'Sir Daniels' on the Oxford and Wolverhampton services.

Armstrong died in harness in 1877, having (so it was said) worked himself to death, and was succeeded by William Dean, who in the year of his appointment produced four rebuilt engines to supplement the Gooch 4-2-2s on the broad gauge. In their original form these had been 4-2-4 tank locomotives built for the Bristol &

Exeter Railway in the last years of its independent existence. They had had flangeless driving wheels of 8 ft 10 in diameter, and one of them was involved in a bad accident which was held in part to be attributable to the fact that the guidance of the engine depended only on the bogie wheels. Dean rebuilt them as 4-2-2 tender locomotives with 8-foot wheels, re-using the former boilers and cylinders, and put them to work on the main line with the Gooch engines. They were unpopular with their crews and were withdrawn one by one, the last surviving until the broad gauge was abolished in 1892.

Dean also built ten more 2-2-2s similar to Armstrong's domeless 'Queens' but having the now unusual feature of outside sandwich framing. It had been found that locomotives so built ran more smoothly on the hard and unyielding 'baulk road' of the broad gauge, and even after the mixed gauge had been introduced one rail of the two was still laid along longitudinal timber baulks. Hence, no doubt, Dean's continuance of a practice no

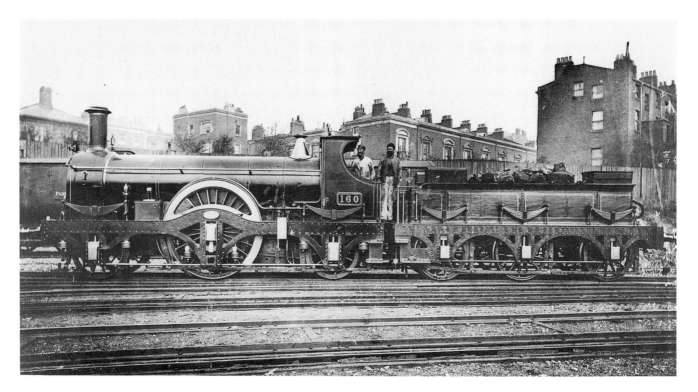

GWR 2-2-2 No. 160, of the 'Queen' class, with domeless boiler and sandwich frames.   (*Photomatic*)

other line then employed. Sandwich framing, however, had its disadvantages—in particular the working loose of the bolts which kept the sandwich together. So these were the last engines to be so constructed. They were very handsome, with polished brass splasher bands, and they too were used for many years on trains from London to Swindon or Wolverhampton.

In 1884 Dean built as an experiment, a solitary single wheeler tank locomotive, in whose brief history comedy and tragedy combine. It was intended for long-distance express running with standard gauge trains, so was given enormous side tanks which extended along both sides for five-sixths of the length of the frames, and which held, so it was said 2,500 gallons of water. (However, precise information about this locomotive was suppressed and only hints and vague memories remained to guide the enquirer.) At either end the locomotive was supported on a four-wheeled bogie, which does not seem to have been anchored very well to the frame; each had Mansell wheels, wooden blocks replacing spokes between hub and rim. The driving wheels were of 7 ft 8 in diameter. The valve gear was outside, driving valves above the cylinders through rocking levers. After completion, and with steam raised, it left Swindon Works for the first time to take the air on the outside tracks; a crowd attended its launching, including Dean himself. Under the eyes of its designer it moved towards the turntable, derailed itself and fell into the pit. Dean walked away without a word. The engine was recovered, got back somehow into the works, was covered with tarpaulins and eventually dismantled.

Three years later it contributed its wheels and valve motion to a newly-built 2-2-2 which bore little resem-

blance to the engine from which it had received spare-part surgery, except in the retention of the outside valve gear and the rocking lever system, which made its side view look distinctly strange. In its rebuilt form it had only a short life, for while it could pull well it could not run fast. In 1890 it underwent a second metamorphosis and emerged as a 7-foot single with outside bearings to all wheels. Nothing of the original engine was now left.

The London, Brighton & South Coast Railway, unlike its other neighbours south of the River Thames, found a use for single wheelers right up to the end of the century and beyond. In 1870 William Stroudley succeeded John Chester Craven as Locomotive Superintendent at Brighton Works, and faced a daunting task, that of reorganizing the locomotive stock from the motley collection left by Craven, concerning whom C. Hamilton Ellis once wrote, in regard to his retirement:
"There may have been some persuasion. Even that patient body of men, the LB&SC Board, was fed up with his chaotic department ... There was many a dry eye in Brighton Locomotive Works on the day when he took his hat down from the peg for the last time."

Stroudley proved to be not only a locomotive designer of genius, who tried as far as he could to introduce standardization, and painted his locomotives in the most attractive livery that any British railway company ever adopted, but was also a friendly and accessible human being; his assistants venerated him and, if they themselves later became Locomotive Superintendents, perpetuated some of his design features in their own engines. When he died prematurely in France in 1889, of an illness contracted there when he accompanied his exhibition locomotive, the 0-4-2 'Gladstone' *Edward Blount*, to Paris, his demise was genuinely mourned.

He is of course principally known for his 'Gladstones', but he built a number of 2-2-2s, beginning in 1874 with No. 151 (later No. 326) *Grosvenor*. This has claims to be the most handsome engine of that wheel arrangement ever built, with the possible exception of Dugald Drummond's two locomotives built for the North British Railway, to be mentioned later. It had 6 ft 9 in driving wheels, the largest he ever used on any engine, and was the first British locomotive of its kind to be fitted with the Westinghouse air-brake, whose pump was tucked tidily away behind the right-hand splasher. This engine contrasts interestingly with the GWR 'Queens' in its general dimensions, being rather less powerful but having a slightly larger boiler. When new it was fitted with huge wooden brake-shoes acting on the driving and trailing wheels; these were later replaced with cast iron ones. *Grosvenor* was popular with its drivers, and in 1875 had the honour of heading a Royal special between Victoria and Portsmouth, carrying the Prince and Princess of Wales. It averaged 48 mph over a difficult road, which was something the Queen herself would never have permitted; 40 mph was the maximum allowable by any train in which she travelled. *Grosvenor* lasted until 1907, when it was sold for scrap. It deserved a better fate.

LBSCR Stroudley 2-2-2 No. 326 *Grosvenor*, with 6 ft 9 in driving wheels, at Eastbourne.   (*Burtt Collection, NRM*)

In 1877 Stroudley built a second single wheeler of the same style, slightly smaller—No. 325 *Abergavenny*. It had driving wheels of 6 ft 6 in diameter, the largest he normally used. It worked the Newhaven boat trains for several years before being relegated to semi-fast or branch line duties, and lasted until 1909.

Following his cautious 'toes in the water first' introduction of this type, Stroudley went on to build as many as 24 of his Class G 2-2-2s, beginning in 1880. They closely resembled the previous two, and had, like *Abergavenny*, 6 ft 6 in driving wheels. They had metal brake-shoes from the beginning. With larger cylinders they were a little more powerful than *Grosvenor*, and were very much liked by their crews. For a long while they had the Portsmouth line expresses to themselves, and coped well with the admittedly light trains over the steep gradients between Sutton and Horsham. Not until 1895 were they displaced by 4-4-0s. For a while one of them, No. 329 *Stephenson*, was selected to haul the "Eastbourne Sunday Pullman" from and to Victoria. Withdrawals began in 1907 and by 1914 the class was extinct.

It may seem surprising that on a line like the LBSCR, with its many severe banks, some as steep as 1 in 80, Stroudley should have built so many single wheelers. In explanation it should be emphasized that the banks were generally short, that schedules were by no means exacting, and that in any case no locomotive longer than a six-wheeler could be accommodated on the short turntables which existed in his time, some of which were so situated that enlargement was difficult, although eventually it had to be done.

Dugald Drummond, who had been closely associated

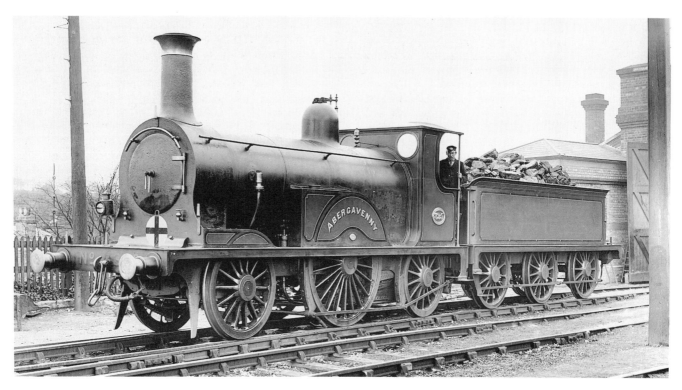

LBSCR Stroudley 2-2-2 No. 325 *Abergavenny*, with 6 ft 6 in driving wheels, at Tunbridge Wells.   (*Burtt Collection, NRM*)

LBSCR Stroudley 2-2-2 No. 333 *Connaught*, with slightly larger cylinders than *Abergavenny*, but otherwise similar.

(*Burtt Collection, NRM*)

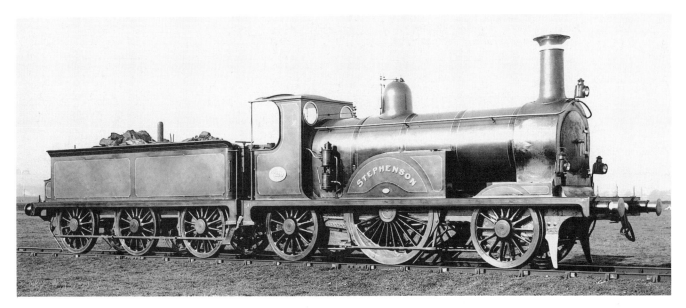

LBSCR Stroudley 2-2-2 No. 329 *Stephenson*, the last of its class to be withdrawn, in May 1914.   (*Burtt Collection, NRM*)

with Stroudley, both on the Highland and LBSC railways, moved from Brighton in 1875 to the North British Railway to replace Thomas Wheatley as Locomotive Superintendent. The latter, like Craven at Brighton, had been under pressure to resign his post, but not because his department had been in a muddle, but because he was suspected of malversation of funds. He went off to manage a tiny railway in the south-west of Scotland for the remainder of his life, and Drummond, succeeding him, now had the opportunity for the first time to design a locomotive to operate express trains between Berwick-on-Tweed and Glasgow by way of Edinburgh.

As might have been expected, the engine he produced closely resembled Stroudley's *Grosvenor*, constructed two years previously at Brighton, even to the extent of

including large wooden brake-blocks working on the driving and trailing wheels. The only noticeable differences, apart from the liveries, were the shape of the cab roof, the use of Ramsbottom, instead of Salter, safety valves on the dome, which was a little further forward than on Stroudley's engine though still set on the second ring of the boiler, and the rather more prominent outside brake rodding. Dimensionally the two designs were very similar, but the NBR engines were a little heavier and had greater adhesion weight. The tractive efforts were the same. One, No. 474, was named

NBR Drummond 2-2-2 No. 475 *Berwick*, built by Neilson & Co. in 1875. The similarity in appearance and details to Stroudley's *Grosvenor* is remarkable. Drummond had been Stroudley's assistant until coming to Cowlairs as Locomotive Superintendent in 1875, hence the resemblance. Note the huge wooden brake-blocks.

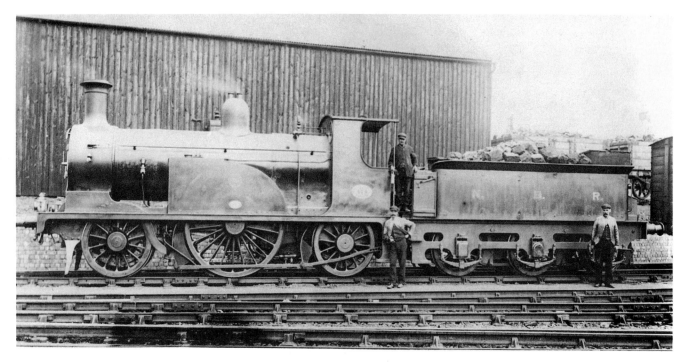

North British Railway Drummond 2-2-2 No. 474, originally named *Glasgow*. The name was removed when it was re-boilered.   (*Photomatic*)

Glasgow, the other, No. 475, *Berwick*, the extremes on the line on which most of their work was done.

Details of how they performed are lacking, but they were expected to keep time on a 70-minute schedule between Glasgow (Queen Street) and Edinburgh (Waverley), 47.2 miles which included the one mile ascent of Cowlairs bank at 1 in 41, formerly rope-assisted, but now having rear-end banking help from the engine which had brought the coaches into the terminus. Both engines lasted nearly as long as their designer, and were never rebuilt; they were withdrawn in 1910.

As noticed in Chapter 1, the Great Eastern Railway was already operating many of its fast passenger trains with 2-2-2s which dated from 1862. When S. W. Johnson succeeded Sinclair as Locomotive Superintendent at Stratford he made the experiment of rebuilding two of them with front bogies. Five years later, however, neither the rebuilt nor the unrebuilt singles were any longer equal to the task of hauling the GER expresses; a larger and more powerful type was needed. Johnson's successor, Massey Bromley, designed a 4-2-2 of which ten were built in 1879 by Dübs & Co. of Glasgow and ten more during 1881/2 by Kitson & Co.

The influence of Stirling's 8-footers was apparent in the shape of the radially-slotted driving splashers and the

GER 4-2-2 No. 246, designed by Massey Bromley in 1879. Note the manner in which a single lever operates the braking upon the driving and trailing wheels on either side, thus doing away with the need for brake rodding.   (*NRM*)

MSLR 2-2-2 No. 507, designed by C. Sacré in 1882. Note the unusually placed side window in the cab.　　*(Photomatic)*

curve of the running plates over the outside cranks; the driving wheels, however, were of 7 ft 6 in diameter and the outside cylinders had a shorter stroke than did Stirling's engines. Special features were the long wheelbase of the bogie, the rather un-ornamental stovepipe chimney, the placing of the valves above the cylinders, worked by inside valve gear through rocking shafts, and the placing of forward-facing doors on either side of the cab to give the driver direct access to the running boards.

These engines apparently gave every satisfaction in practice, although no detailed records of their running exist. Ahrons notes two things about them:

"The writer, when standing on a wayside platform, sometimes remarked the lateral swaying motion of these engines when they were running at high speeds, which was in the nature of a gentle movement of long amplitude, very unlike the short and sharp jerky motion of the L&NWR outside-cylinder 2-2-2 engines of the 'Lady of the Lake' class, with short wheelbase and no bogie. Another characteristic of the GER engines was the astonishing manner in

MSLR 2-2-2 No. 104. Note the number painted on the side instead of a metal number-plate, and the slightly larger cab; also the raised firebox casing to which Sacré was partial.

(Photomatic)

which they could climb the Bethnal Green bank out of Liverpool Street with fifteen and sixteen six-wheeled coaches, frequently without slipping . . ."

Some of these engines were later altered by Bromley's successor, James Holden, who gave them new and slightly smaller cylinders with inside valves worked directly from the eccentrics on the driving axle.

Last to be noticed in the period under review in this chapter are the twelve outside-cylindered 2-2-2s designed by Charles Sacré and built at Gorton Works, Manchester, for the Manchester, Sheffield & Lincolnshire Railway—which, 15 years later, after putting out an extension to London, became the Great Central Railway. Built during 1882/3, these engines were the last outside-cylindered 2-2-2s to be constructed in Great Britain, and had a distinctly old-fashioned look. The piston and connecting rods were partly hidden behind valances that extended backwards to form crank splashers. The cylinders were fairly large, the driving wheels had a diameter of 7 ft 6 in, the leading and trailing wheels had axleboxes in outside framing, and the raised firebox top provided a slightly archaic touch. The short wheelbase made for jerky running at speed. They did not look like greyhounds but were nevertheless given a short spell on fast trains when selected to take on the Manchester expresses from King's Cross when they had reached Retford. These trains were light, but between Sheffield and Manchester there were the tremendous gradients on either side of Woodhead Tunnel to be climbed. After 1887 they were transferred to work the Cheshire Lines Committee's services between Manchester and Liverpool, some of which had quite tight timings. E. L. Ahrons noted their ability to get away rapidly from stops, and he suspected that the weights on their driving wheels were greater than the published figures suggested.

✳ ✳ ✳

Quite a number of records of the running of the GNR single wheelers can be found in early issues of *The Railway Magazine*, although they principally date from the early years of the present century. E. L. Ahrons also mentions some earlier runs. Most deal with the 8-footers and the 7 ft 7$\frac{1}{2}$ in singles, but the writer has been able to find one example of the work of a 7-footer of the 1868 batch in one of Ahrons' articles, when he timed No. 55, with a load of 180 tons, in great detail, recording the time at every milepost between Grantham and Retford. The schedule was rather a slow one, 42 minutes, on which 1$\frac{1}{2}$ minutes were gained despite a signal check on the approach to Retford. On the downhill stretch before and through Newark the mile-a-minute rate was maintained, with a maximum of 64$\frac{1}{2}$ mph being twice reached; beyond that speed fell away gradually to 41$\frac{1}{2}$ mph at Markham Summit and then rose to 57 before the Retford check. With such a small locomotive this was not bad going; Ahrons thought it 'distinguished', but

that is perhaps to claim too much.

With the 8-footers Ahrons had several runs but did not always time them. On an occasion when he did he was rewarded by a good performance behind No. 773 on an 'up' Manchester express when the load, as usual, was a mere 90 tons. King's Cross was reached from Grantham in 116 minutes, 44 mph having been attained at the top of the rise to Stoke and 75 at Little Bytham. After the slack through Peterborough speed rose to 63$\frac{1}{4}$ mph on the level stretch beyond, fell away to a minimum of 48$\frac{1}{2}$ up Abbots Ripton bank and reached 66$\frac{1}{2}$ beyond Huntingdon. The minimum speed at the St Neots hump was 56 mph, and 61 was attained near Tempsford; beyond Biggleswade it had fallen to 50, but there was a recovery to 55$\frac{1}{2}$ and then a gradual fall to 44 at Stevenage Summit. Beyond Welwyn it rose to 66$\frac{3}{4}$, at Potters Bar it was 52$\frac{1}{4}$, and speed had risen again to 63$\frac{1}{4}$ when the train was checked by signals. Times from the Grantham start were 31 min 3 sec to Peterborough, 50 min 21 sec to Huntingdon, 79 min 5 sec to Hitchin, and the arrival at King's Cross was a minute early. The train was on time throughout the journey and no attempt was made to run early; the run may be regarded as typical.

The best-known performances of both the 8-footers and the 7 ft 7$\frac{1}{2}$ in 2-2-2s are of course the runs made with the racing trains in 1888 and 1895. During the 'Race to Edinburgh' in August 1888 the times from King's Cross to Grantham tended to decrease as the load decreased, and on 25th August the journey, with a load of 105 tons, was done in the same number of minutes—due, it would seem, to energetic uphill running. Only one complete log exists, recorded by Rev. W. J. Scott on the last day of the race, when Potters Bar was passed in 17 min 25 sec, Hitchin in 35 min 25 sec, Peterborough in 77 min 27 sec and Stoke signal box, the summit point, in 104 min 42 sec. After a fast finish Grantham was reached in 110 min 2 sec. These times do not indicate any very fast downhill running. Quicker times were made in the 'Race to Aberdeen' in 1895, the best being when Driver Falkinder, with No. 668 hauling 101 tons, passed Potters Bar in the astonishing time of 15 minutes, Hitchin in 33 minutes, Peterborough in 72 minutes and Stoke in 96 minutes; a very rapid finish brought the train into Grantham in 102 minutes. (The times were taken to the nearest half-minute.) Earlier in the race one of the 2-2-2s with a train of 146 tons reached York from Grantham in 85 min 10 sec, attaining 74$\frac{1}{2}$ mph near Claypole; a signal check before Doncaster preventing an 'even time' arrival at York.

During the first decade of the following century, when both types were approaching old age, Rous-Marten recorded some sparkling performances. On an 'up' express from Leeds, with 100 tons, an 8-footer (he does not say which one) reached King's Cross in 108 min 12 sec, despite three signal checks, the net time being 105 minutes—well up to the standard of the earlier racing performances. On another occasion he timed the now preserved No. 1, with a load of 200 tons, when the 50$\frac{1}{2}$ miles from Grantham to Doncaster were covered in 51$\frac{1}{2}$

GNR 4-2-2 Stirling 8-footer No. 1 on a train near New Barnet. Note that the front brake pipe has now been added, after increasing train loads compelled occasional piloting.
(*Photomatic*)

minutes, the maximum speed being 72 mph somewhere near Newark, with a subsequent minimum of 50 at Markham. Perhaps the most meritorious of these later performances was when No. 667, on the 1.30 pm from King's Cross, took a 276-ton load from Peterborough to Doncaster in only $1\frac{1}{2}$ minutes over the booked time of 92 minutes for the $79\frac{1}{2}$ miles, despite the handicap of a strong side wind—minimum speeds were $37\frac{3}{4}$ mph at Stoke and 41 at Markham.

At about the same time he also experienced, on one of the short-lived "Manchester Flyers", a very praiseworthy effort by a 7 ft $7\frac{1}{2}$ in 2-2-2, No. 877, with a light load of about 100 tons, from Sheffield to King's Cross. A string of signal checks caused time to be lost to Retford, but the engine, once on its own main line, ran vigorously, reaching 56 mph on the rise to Askham and then accelerating to 74 before slowing to pick up water at Muskham troughs. Picking up speed rapidly to $62\frac{1}{2}$ at Claypole, and passing Grantham still doing 60, No. 877 topped the rise to Stoke at 55 and then started going all out down the bank beyond, until checked by signals beyond Little Bytham. A speed of $75\frac{1}{2}$ mph was then attained on the level before another slowing to pick up water from Werrington troughs. Peterborough was passed at the usual 10 mph; speed then rose to 75 at the foot of Abbots Ripton bank, which was ascended at a minimum of 56. Beyond Huntingdon the maximum was $76\frac{1}{4}$, and speed remained high enough beyond to give

Rous-Marten cause to hope that it might not fall below 60 at Stevenage; however, a check before Hitchin brought the rate down to 10 mph, so his hopes were dashed. However, the train was on time and there was now no point in hurrying. King's Cross was reached nearly three minutes early, in 172 min 17 sec from Sheffield, the net time being about 160 minutes for the 162 miles.

In regard to the enlarged 8-footers of 1894/5, Rous-Marten mentions a run made by No 1006 in 1896 between Grantham and York, $82\frac{1}{2}$ miles, in $80\frac{1}{2}$ minutes, with a load of 200 tons. It is a pity that he did not publish a full record of this run, which with such a load was very good indeed.

As to the GWR single wheelers mentioned earlier in this chapter, a few reports of their performance exist—in one case a very full one. Ahrons mentions a run behind one of the 'sandwich frame' 2-2-2s, recorded between 1885 and 1892—he does not say exactly when. No. 166, with a load of 100 tons, gained $2\frac{1}{4}$ minutes on schedule between Oxford and Leamington, covering the $43\frac{1}{2}$ miles in $48\frac{3}{4}$ minutes and reaching a maximum of $70\frac{1}{2}$ mph approaching Leamington. On another occasion No. 1000, a rebuilt 'Queen' with a raised Belpaire firebox and large dome, ran from Oxford to Birmingham, $65\frac{3}{4}$ miles, in 69 minutes with a load of 120 tons as far as Leamington, one 20-ton coach then being slipped. This represented a gain of ten minutes on schedule.

The most fully recorded achievement of one of these old engines, however, was that described by Rous-Marten in *The Engineer* of 4th November 1898. No. 162 *Cobham*, a rebuilt 'Sir Daniel', with six bogie coaches and one six-wheeler, weighing in all 160 tons, managed, despite serious checks en route, to gain over nine minutes on the 147-minute schedule from Paddington to Birmingham, Snow Hill. In his own words:

"The weather was perfect, being fine and bright without a breath of wind. The rails were dry throughout. Starting from Paddington with absolute punctuality according to the station clock . . . it soon became evident that the driver, Hughes, who managed his engine from first to last with admirable skill and judgement, was determined to get as much as possible in hand from the beginning. Each station was passed in the quickest time within my personal experience on that railway; thus by the time we reached Twyford we were just one second better than the mile-a-minute average, the 31 miles having taken 30 min 59 sec. Reading (36 miles) was passed in 35 min 29 sec—a record so far as my own travelling over that ground is concerned.

But we speedily had to pay for being in advance of time. After a bad check near Scours Lane Junction we were brought to a dead stand by signals at Tilehurst, the $38\frac{3}{4}$ miles from London having been run in 38 min 20 sec from start to stop, or at the average rate of 60.6 miles an hour. After a stoppage of 2 min 21 sec we proceeded on our way, having lost 5 min 20 sec by the check and stop, including the extra start and stop. It may be noted that the engine managed to maintain a steady speed of 64.8 miles an hour up the continuous slight ascent of 1 in 1320 between Maidenhead and Twyford. No. 162 continued to fly along bravely, and Oxford, $63\frac{1}{2}$ miles, was passed in 64 min 3 sec actual running time from Paddington, or 61 min 4 sec net. Here permanent way repairs compelled a special slowing to 12 miles an hour in lieu of the usual authorised 40. Two miles further on another reduction of speed for relaying caused a loss of 72 seconds. At Somerton, $78\frac{1}{4}$ miles, adverse signals were again encountered, and after a preliminary slackening we came to a dead halt for 3 min 40 sec, the distance, a mile further than to Swindon, having been done in 79 min 17 sec running time, or 75 min 6 sec net.

By this time all hope of a fine run seemed to have departed; nevertheless so smartly did Hughes work his good old engine, and so briskly did Cobham respond to his efforts, that Leamington, 106 miles, was actually passed in 1 hr 53 min 49 sec inclusive time from London, or in 1 hr 47 min 48 sec . . . actual travelling time. The net running, deducting carefully ascertained delays, was only 100 min 18 sec, allowing nothing for the extra slowing through Oxford. Speed was reduced to 25 miles an hour through Leamington, and had not been fully recovered when the Hatton bank, much at 1 in 105, was faced. Unfortunately during the ascent another slackening for relaying had to be made, the reduced speed being continued for a full mile. Notwithstanding this the 4 miles 13 chains from Warwick to Hatton occupied only 5 min 47 sec.

Our troubles now were over, and we experienced no further hindrances, escaping even the check so frequently encountered at Bordesley, and in approaching Snow Hill station. We pulled up at the Birmingham platform at 11.48 exactly by the station clock . . . The run of 129 miles 25 chains from Paddington had thus been made in 2 hr 18 min 9 sec, including two dead stoppages amounting in all to 6 min 1 sec. Thus the actual travelling time was only 2 hr 12 min 8 sec, or at the average rate of 58.7 miles an hour, allowing nothing for the two extra startings and stoppings, or for the bad slowings near Oxford and Hatton, which together involved an absolute loss of 8 min 34 sec carefully ascertained. If this loss be deducted from the actual travelling time . . . it leaves the net time 123 min 34 sec for the $129\frac{1}{4}$ miles.

One must agree that this was a good run, whose merit was only equalled by its describer's verbosity; he was presumably paid according to the length of his article.

No records seem to have remained of how the Stroudley and Drummond 2-2-2s performed on the LBSCR and NBR. On the GER Massey Bromley's 4-2-2s did not have much opportunity to show their paces, schedules being very easy. Ahrons recorded a run with a light train in 1885 when four minutes were gained with ease between Cambridge and Liverpool Street, though the speed nowhere reached 60 miles an hour. On another occasion, over the level line between Lincoln and Spalding, the $38\frac{1}{4}$ miles were covered in $45\frac{3}{4}$ minutes by No. 600, hauling ten coaches, about 150 tons; again, no speeds of 60 mph were reached.

On the Manchester, Sheffield & Lincolnshire Railway, Sacré's singles did some respectable work, especially when on foreign metals. For a while they headed the GNR Manchester expresses over the northern part of their journey from and to Grantham, running on the latter's main line between Grantham and Retford. Ahrons mentions a run in which, with a mere 84 tons load, No. 500 was opened out going southwards after Retford, speed rising to 55 mph up Gamston bank, and to 72 on the subsequent descent to the crossing of the River Trent before Newark; over two minutes were gained between Sheffield and Grantham.

After they had been transferred to the Cheshire Lines Committee's metals the singles dealt successfully with the Manchester and Liverpool service's trains so long as they were not given more than about 120 tons to haul. Ahrons gives two instances of their work here, one when, with 100 tons, $1\frac{1}{4}$ minutes were gained on the 40-minute non-stop schedule, and the other of a train of 140 tons which stopped intermediately at Warrington and was allowed five minutes more; on this occasion a little time was lost because of a bad permanent way slack. The locomotive in both cases was No. 506. As will be seen in a subsequent chapter, this stretch of line was used as a kind of retirement meadow for single wheelers when no use could be found for them elsewhere.

* * * * * *

3 The Irish Great Northern Single Wheelers of 1885

The year 1885, as will be seen in the next chapter, was a critical one in the history of the single wheeler, when from being the express type of the past it became that of the immediate future. In that year, too, a locomotive type appeared in Ireland, of which two were built, and which looked both backwards and forwards. It was the first inside-cylindered bogie single wheeler to be built for service in these islands, but it lacked the device, not yet invented, which all subsequent similar engines were to possess—a means of forcing sand under the driving wheels instead of merely dropping it in front of them.

The Irish Great Northern Railway, in common with all the other Irish railway companies, did not at that time go in for speed. There was no particular demand for it. Ireland did not harbour thrusting tycoons who regretted every moment that could not be actively given to business and money-making. It was a rural land where people were mostly content to stay put and did not dash around restlessly visiting relatives and friends, who in any case were mostly within walking or riding distance. It was well supplied with railways—far more so than at present—but these were run economically, which in general meant slowly. Only the lines between Dublin and Belfast, and Dublin and Cork, were double-tracked throughout; those to Derry, Sligo and Galway were single for a great deal of their length, and single track imposed its own limitations on the speeds which could be run because of the need to exchange tokens and to reduce speed when negotiating passing loops. However, the line linking Dublin with Belfast, Ireland's two largest cities, as well as that between London and Cork, did run the fastest, or at any rate the least slow, trains in what was then (in Bernard Shaw's phrase) "John Bull's other island". It has to be admitted that such celerity as they did possess was largely owing to pressure from the Post Office in London.

The Great Northern of Ireland's main line from Amiens Street terminus in Dublin to Great Victoria Street in Belfast passed through three sizeable centres of population: Drogheda, whence a branch diverged up the Boyne valley to Oldcastle; Dundalk, the site of the company's locomotive and carriage works, where one changed for Enniskillen, Bundoran, Strabane and Derry; and Portadown, whence the main line from Belfast to Derry diverged. With all its branch lines, though the system was smaller in extent than that of the Great Southern & Western, it served more people. Its best express was the early morning Mail train from Dublin to Belfast, whose timings had to be agreed with the Postmaster General in London, since the Post Office provided a subsidy towards the maintenance of a rapid and punctual postal service—a subsidy which from time to time required to be re-negotiated at the cost of a good deal of haggling, the Post Office authorities being notoriously close-fisted. Until 1882 the Mail trains took $3\frac{1}{4}$ hours between the two chief cities, stopping only at Drogheda, Dundalk and Portadown, but in that year it was accelerated by ten minutes. It had to be a fast service—fast in contemporary Irish terms—since nearly all the letters between England and the north of Ireland went that way, by the Holyhead–Kingstown packet boat. There had recently been protests from the Belfast business community that it was not fast enough, and requests had been made for a second Mail route by way of Stranraer and Larne (which were actually acceded to). Hence the accelerations.

A timing of just over three hours, while nearly as fast as Ireland could offer anywhere else, was not exactly brilliant. An average speed of $37\frac{3}{4}$ mph over the first stage, $38\frac{1}{2}$ over the second, 37 over the third and $39\frac{1}{2}$ over the fourth, was well below contemporary standards in England, where the English Great Northern was then running the $105\frac{1}{2}$ miles in both directions between King's Cross and Grantham in under the two hours with its lighter Leeds expresses. Even the heavier Scottish-bound trains did not take much longer—50 mph-plus was their standard. But there was this difference: when the "Flying Scotsman" left King's Cross at 10 am each weekday morning, that was when it did leave; it did not have to wait. The morning Mail train from Amiens Street frequently *did* have to wait. Bad weather might cause the English mails to arrive late at Kingstown. The business community in Belfast, however, still expected their letters from England to arrive on time. So the Mail train might have to run faster than its advertised booking in order to make up lost time. The practice was for it to be held for a certain period. If by then the mails had not arrived it was dispatched and expected to recover some of the delay en route. If the mails then managed to reach Amiens Street a little while later, a special train would be sent on, made up of two coaches and hauled by an ancient single wheeler with 5 ft 7 in driving wheels, to overtake the Mail at Dundalk and there transfer the precious bags.

So the locomotive set apart for working the Mail trains had to be capable of reaching Belfast in very much less than the time officially allowed. It might be necessary to recover time not only after the agreed delay but sometimes also after a second wait at Dundalk for the Postal Special to catch it up. The latter, too, might have to run fast, a requirement to which its small wheels do not seem to have been a hindrance. The following is quoted from a letter sent to the author by an Irish friend, who did some train-timing during the days of steam and knew the route well:

"If the Special was not too far behind, the Limited might be held in Dundalk for it; then the Specials did run hard. L. J. Watson, who was Chief Draughtsman at Dundalk, 1892–1933, and no doubt travelled on them, told me the little engines sometimes did the $22\frac{1}{2}$ miles from Drogheda to Dundalk in 22 minutes, which I don't believe, comparing it with a 22-minute run I once timed behind a 4-4-0 with an 83 ton train. It involved accelerating from 50 to 59 up

3¾ miles of 1 in 176 and running at 77 to 82 over the next 13 miles, mostly downhill. But it does show the old singles ran hard—they might have done it in 23 minutes or so."

In 1880 J. C. Park, Patrick Stirling's Chief Draughtsman at Doncaster and his right-hand man for many years, and who had helped in the designing and construction of the GNR 8-footers, was appointed to the newly established post of Locomotive Superintendent at Dundalk, and brought with him Doncaster traditions, though he did not apply them slavishly. Soon after his arrival he had to consider the question of providing special engines to work the Dublin and Belfast Mails. Single wheelers of the kind mentioned above had already been used on the fastest trains between the two cities, although as long as three different companies were involved none of them worked through over the whole distance.

In 1880 an ancient 2-2-2, No. 15, originally constructed by Beyer, Peacock & Co. of Manchester to one of their standard designs supplied to British and Continental railways, and having 6-foot driving wheels, had been rebuilt with a longer wheelbase and a larger firebox and put to work on the Dublin–Belfast expresses, running through without any change. The rebuilding was considerable, practically resulting in a new engine. Schedules had not then been improved to the 3 hr 5 mins standard, but the Post Office was pushing for a quicker timing which was clearly going to have to be introduced; hence the experimental rebuilding. Park decided on a new design to cope with the new situation. Among the engines that he constructed, besides 4-4-0s for ordinary passenger work, were two 4-2-2s specifically intended for working the Mail trains. They were the last single wheelers to be built for service in Ireland and the only ones of this wheel arrangement ever to work there.

In September 1883 the order was placed with Beyer, Peacock & Co. It is not known to what extent Park was responsible for the details of the design. In all probability the specification just gave a general indication of the sort of locomotive required and the dimensional parameters. In two respects it departed from contemporary Doncaster practice—the co-existence of a front bogie with inside cylinders, and the provision of a steam dome instead of a perforated pipe for steam collection.

The only features which were definitely reminiscent of Doncaster were the chimney and cab, the latter being like the Stirling type but having curved cut-aways at either side and a roof that extended backwards. The finished locomotive, as it appears in photographs, looks rather a midget. The boiler was 1½ feet shorter than the one carried by Stirling's 8-footers. The total heating surface was also smaller, as also were the cylinders. The declared adhesion weight was 14 tons[1] as compared with the 8-footers' 15 to 17 tons. The tractive effort, on the usual assumption that 85 per cent of the working pressure of 140 lbs per square inch was effective in the cylinders, was only about 8,500 lbs, as compared with the 12,000 to 13,000 lbs of the Stirling engines. Yet these

locomotives had to be able to tackle gradients much harder than any on the GNR main line in England; there are long stretches at 1 in 100 and even steeper on both sides of the summit near Adavoyle in the foothills of the Mourne Mountains. Only with a light load could so small an engine have done it. However, the loads *were* light, the usual rake of coaches in 1885, and for some years afterwards, being five six-wheelers, four (including the Post Office van), for Belfast and one for Derry, the latter being detached at Portadown—some 60 tons, lessening to under 50 tons. Even during the racing month of August 1895, Stirling's engines had to haul heavier loads than that. So time recovery was no doubt possible.

The names on the two locomotives, Nos 88 and 89, *Victoria* and *Albert*, were not in accordance with the GNR(I)'s usual naming policy, which until that time had been, curiously, to name only freight engines, which were called after places in Ireland served by the GNR system.[2] One imagines, too, that the names given to these two engines would not have been approved by those with Republican sympathies (of whom there were then a few) though Home Rulers would probably not have minded.

Great Northern Railway of Ireland 4-2-2s Nos 88 and 89, *Victoria* and *Albert* (as built)

Date ordered:	1883
Date delivered:	1885
Builders:	Beyer, Peacock & Co.
Boiler – length:	9 ft 11¾ in
	(10 ft 3¼ in to throatplate)
width:	4 ft 0¾ in (average of 3 rings)
tubes:	164 of 2-inch diameter
Firebox:	4 ft 4 in by 4 ft 6 in
Grate area:	14.84 sq ft
Total heating surface:	966.7 sq ft
Boiler pressure:	140 lbs per sq in
Cylinders:	16 in × 22 in
	(16½ in × 22 in when rebuilt)
Wheels – bogie:	3 ft 1½ in
driving:	6 ft 7 in
trailing:	3 ft 7½ in
Total wheelbase:	18 ft 11½ in
Weight of engine in working order:	34 tons
Published adhesion weight:	14 tons
Tender – coal:	2 tons
water:	1,700 galls (2,000 galls when rebuilt in 1892)
Weight of tender in working order:	22 tons 2 cwt

1. This was the published figure, but much could be done by the unofficial adjustment of springing, and it seems likely that the true adhesion figure was more like 15¾ tons. The same sort of deception was practised on this side of the Irish Sea—as already indicated, Stirling himself offended in this respect.
2. Could the disinclination to name passenger locomotives in this way have been in case travellers might think the train was going to the place so-named? Names of this sort were removed from some British engines for that reason.

GNR(I) 4-2-2 No. 89 *Albert*, as built by Beyer, Peacock & Co. in 1885, in photographic grey before shipment to Ireland. Note the railway company's monogram on the splasher.   (*Greater Manchester Museum of Science and Technology*)

4-2-2 No. 88 *Victoria*, at Dundalk in GNR(I) livery.   (*H. Fayle courtesy Irish Railway Record Society*)

The Queen and her Consort had been well received in the country nearly forty years earlier, when they had paid special visits to Cork and Dublin from the Royal Yacht to show their sympathy with the people, after the potato famine had wreaked its deadly ravages. Possibly the names on this occasion were bestowed with the forthcoming Golden Jubilee in mind.

The nameplates were not placed on the sides of the boilers, as was customary on the GNR, but along the curved edges of the splashers, in small neat lettering which would scarcely have been legible at any distance; the numbers on the cab sides were more distinct. The large sand-boxes dropped their contents by gravity. However, the invention of steam sanding in England, as mentioned in the next chapter, caused this apparatus to be introduced on Irish lines also, and in 1888 both locomotives were appropriately modified. The framing and springing were internal, with plate springs for the bogie and driving wheels and coil springs for the rear carrying wheels. The cylinder diameters were slightly increased when re-boring became necessary. In 1890, after the accident near Armagh when unsatisfactory braking caused a train to run backwards downhill and crash, with the loss of many lives, the engines, in common with all others, were fitted with automatic vacuum brakes.

These two locomotives ran the Mail trains in both directions, on the 3-hour timing, for about ten years, and were only very rarely put on other duties. From mileage figures which have been preserved it seems likely that they took turns, a week at a time, on the Mail trains, with each having its stint extended when the other was away for repair. In 1895, however, the train increased in weight, bogie stock replacing the six-wheelers, and this is probably the reason why the singles were then taken off this duty and replaced by newer 4-4-0s built by Park's successor, Clifford. They were withdrawn in 1904. It is sometimes said that they were rebuilt into 4-4-0s, but this is not correct, though elements of them may have been employed in later engines; the bogies probably being re-used.

One may end with a note of what they looked like. The livery was Brunswick green, lined with black bands edged in white. The chimney and smokebox were black, as were the visible parts of the framing and the rims of the wheels. The driving wheel splashers had double brass strips parallel to their edges, enclosing a crimson lake band on which were the names in brass letters. The sides of the running boards were in crimson lake; the buffer beams were in vermilion. Wheel spokes, like the rest of the engine, were in green. The company's coat of arms adorned the centre of each splasher.

4 A Fresh Lease of Life

In 1885, as already noted, only five railways were still using single wheelers on their fastest trains, and only one line, the Great Northern, used them and nothing else. However, there was general agreement that if loads could be kept within the limit of a single wheeler's capacity, that type was the one to be preferred. It was simpler and therefore cheaper to construct. It had fewer moving parts and therefore expended less energy in overcoming frictional resistance. It ran more smoothly since there were fewer masses of heavy metal moving to and fro or up and down. In the words of E. L. Ahrons, "no locomotive engineer of that day would have employed a coupled express engine had he been convinced that a single engine was always reliable."

The coupled engine, in the days when steel could not be made sufficiently hard, had the disadvantage that its coupling rods sometimes bent under the strain of alternate pulls and pushes on their crank pins several times a second. Coupled wheels were more difficult to balance. Nor did they wear out at the same rate in the same locomotive. To quote Ahrons again:

"Though it is true that the lighter and less massive engines of those days required the balancing of a larger proportion of the reciprocating masses than is necessary for heavy modern engines, nevertheless there was too great a variation of rail load, estimated as a percentage of the static weight on the driving wheels, which was then only about 11 to 13 tons. The result of this variation may be slight slipping through part of the revolution of the wheels, thus producing flats on the driving tyres, and thereby throwing further stress on the coupling rods. Other things being equal, and within the limits of the adhesion available, the coupled engine gave a lower ratio of effective to indicated horse-power than the single. In addition there was the expense of and loss in re-turning the tyres of two pairs of wheels to the diameter of the smallest wheel, a point of considerable importance owing to the comparatively rapid wear of the soft tyres."

In Great Britain no carefully controlled tests were ever made to determine just how much the internal resistances of two locomotives, similar in all respects except that one had single driving wheels and the other coupled wheels, might differ. Towards the end of the century the more thorough-going Germans *did* carry out such a test, and it was found that when the coupling rods were removed from a 4-4-0 express engine, and it was allowed to coast down a 1 in 200 incline without steam, the coasting speed reached when acceleration ceased was 31.7 mph, whereas when the experiment was tried again with the coupling rods in position the coasting speed was only 24.8 mph. This suggested that the coupling rods were responsible for about 20 per cent of the total frictional resistance. Had the test been made thirty years earlier, when softer steel would have been used, the percentage might well have been higher.

So what Patrick Stirling felt in his bones about the disadvantages of using coupled wheels in an express engine may have been partly justified—at any rate when he began to build his 8-footers. By 1885, however, things were beginning to change. Harder steels could now be had for use in bearings, tyres and rails, with a resultant lessening of friction and greater resistance to strains and stresses.

Meanwhile, on many lines the 2-4-0 was replacing the single wheeler. The Midland, as noted in Chapter 1, built no more of the latter after 1866, and in 1884 an order went out from Derby Works that, because of their propensity for slipping, all single wheelers were to be withdrawn from use and laid up. Many were used as stationary steam boilers here and there over the MR system; others were just covered up and left alone.

One MR official, however, regretted this decision. This was Robert Weatherburn, at that time District Locomotive Superintendent at Leicester. Born with railways in his blood—his father had been an associate of George and Robert Stephenson—he had had a varied career as a railway official which included service on German and Russian lines, about which he had much to say in a series of autobiographical articles published in *The Railway Magazine*. They give the impression of a rather self-important man, much given to self-congratulation, an individualist who regarded trade unions with unreasoning dislike; in one of his articles he recounts his strike-breaking activities with some relish. For locomotives, however, who were obliged to withhold their labour, he had a soft spot—in particular for the discarded single wheelers. To quote his own words:

"When the decisive step was at last taken which led to the building of the single wheelers, which for long after became so markedly a successful feature between London and Leicester and Nottingham, it was brought about as follows. Several small single wheelers designed by Mr Kirtley had been interdicted by circular instruction from running owing to the numerous delays caused by slipping.

One of these was stationed at Leicester and was solely used for supplying steam to stationary engines at pumping stations while their boilers were undergoing examination or repairs. Being very short of power at this time, I never passed the proscribed and laid-up engine without feeling a strong desire to make use of it in some way or another.

At length the temptation was too great. I had the tarpaulin cover removed, and after examination of the tyres and springs, etc, gave instructions for the driving springs, both inside and out, to be strengthened by the addition of an extra plate; the sand-boxes, somewhat straggling, were brought nearer to the wheels, and pipes trained as closely to the tyres as possible to ensure the sand being delivered to a certainty without being blown away [steam sanders were not then in use]. The alterations were completed the day before Leicester Fair. On that day the traffic is always heavier than usual, despite which I determined to change engines and test the result on the South Leicester section. The engine did well.

I kept it at work for some months, unknown, as I thought, to Mr Johnson [the Locomotive Superintendent at Derby], and had nearly forgotten it, when I received a letter instructing me to take the engine in steam to Derby. Mr Billinton [Johnson's Chief Draughtsman at Derby, later to be Locomotive Superintendent on the LB&SCR in succession to Stroudley] met me on my arrival and informed me privately that my action in violating circular instruction had been known to Mr Johnson for some time, and that the working results had been carefully watched and considered successful, particularly . . . the stopping and starting at difficult places; concluding by saying that Mr Johnson had all but decided to adopt large single wheelers for the Southern Division.

Being thus prepared beforehand, my interview was much facilitated. After an implied admonition re the value of circular instructions, I had to recount all the alterations made, loads taken, etc. He then expressed as his opinion that I had loaded the axle to at least 17 tons. The engine was weighed, resulting in 17 tons 3 cwt being registered. I had no fear of the axle, the brand being Reay's, with no flaw or defect. It was decided, after some further discussion, to continue the engine in service. I strongly advised that a bogie should be part of the equipment of the contemplated engines, which was agreed to."

Weatherburn leaves the impression that his 'blind eye to the telescope' attitude to the circular instruction had triggered off the change in policy, but this was surely not so. It is not clear from his account when the incident occurred, but it may well have been *after* the critical experiments described below which really *did* change Johnson's mind. The crucial problem was, how were the driving wheels to be effectively sanded when necessary? The real saviour of the single wheeler, who obtained a stay of execution for a further generation, was F. C. Holt, then the Works Manager at Derby. It occurred to him that instead of merely arranging for sand to *fall*

ahead of the driving wheels it should be *blown* right into the angles between their rims and the rails. A compressed air jet, suitably placed along each sand-fall pipe (which latter could also have its orifice brought much further towards the point of contact of the wheel with the rail) would achieve the desired end. Since the MR used the compressed air Westinghouse brake, the latter's reservoir was there to be tapped. Some locomotives—not single drivers—which worked on the Settle–Carlisle line, with its long stretches inclined at 1 in 100, were fitted with compressed air sanders, with very satisfactory results.

At this point, however, the Westinghouse Brake Company got to know what was going on, and protested. The compressed air stored in the reservoir, they pointed out, was there to stop trains, not to help start them. The device might drain a reservoir of the pressure needed to apply the brakes, so making an accident possible.

The force behind the sand, however, did not *have* to be compressed air. No one could object to boiler steam being used, so the device was altered to permit this. Johnson then took a hand in the proceedings. He removed the coupling rods from six 2-4-0s, fitted them with steam sanding gear for the driving wheels, and put them to work on the Southern Division. Though now effectively 2-2-2s and not 2-4-0s, they showed up better on the gradients and actually burned less coal. These last two consequences, which no one had foreseen, caused Johnson to build the single wheelers which form the theme of the next chapter. Meanwhile, the steam sanding apparatus was taken up, developed and marketed by the engineering firm of Gresham & Craven, and other lines adopted it for use, not only with single wheelers but with all locomotives.

5 The Midland 'Spinners'

S. W. Johnson's decision to build bogie single wheelers for use on the less steeply graded Midland main lines was first implemented in June 1887 when the initial batch began to emerge from Derby Works. Other batches followed at intervals, alterations in detail, size and power being occasionally made culminating in the magnificent final ten. All in their day ran the chief expresses south of Nottingham and Derby, and some went as far north as Leeds.

The first type and its subsequent variations were all very much alike in appearance—there was a definite 'house style', though the alteration in the driving wheel springs could be easily recognized from 1896 onwards, while the last ten were noticeably larger and had their domes placed further back along the boiler barrel; five of these were also given eight-wheeled tenders. In all, as many as 95 were constructed between 1887 and 1900 one of which has been preserved. They were favourites with their engine crews, light on coal, and the chosen targets of many amateur photographers, both when at rest and in action. In the opinion of many they were the most beautiful locomotives of any kind to have been built anywhere. No doubt beauty is in the eye of the beholder, and other engines have had this distinction claimed for them, but they were indeed good-looking locomotives, and ran as well as they looked.

Although the first 'Spinner'[1] to be built was not chronologically the next bogie single wheeler after the two Irish engines of 1885 already described in Chapter 3, since No. 123 of the Caledonian Railway preceded it by a year, the idea of reverting to the use of singles for the MR's more lightly loaded expresses had been brewing in Johnson's mind for some little while, as recounted in the previous chapter. Great care was taken with the design, and the performances of the locomotives as they came out were keenly watched, alterations being made as experience was gained.

Unlike the 4-4-0 express locomotives that Johnson had built during 1876/7, the new design had outside as well as inside frames, with double bearings for each driving wheel and single outside bearings for the trailing carrying wheels. The 7 ft 4 in driving wheels had underhung plate springs outside the wheel spokes (a pattern later to be altered) while the trailing wheels had overhung exterior plate springs. The running board had a deep valance which hid the tops of the bogie wheels on either side. The leading bogie was of the type pioneered by W. Adams on the London & South Western Railway, its frame having a lateral traverse as well as pivoting on a pin; the wheels on either side were supported on the ends of a single longitudinal inverted plate spring. The steam sand blast was of course fitted, with nozzles that pointed backwards at the driving wheel rims in the earlier engines, but on either side, pointing backwards and forwards, on later ones. The running plate on either side arched in an ogee curve above the outer driving wheel bearing and beneath a closed splasher. The lower part of each cab side beneath the curved cut-away formed a rectangular box, as in most other MR and all London & North Western locomotives.

The boiler was of steel—an innovation in British passenger engines, iron boilers having previously been used. It was of the MR's 'D' class, of three rings, with its centre pitched 7 ft 5 in above rail level. The dome, on the second ring and a little forward from the tops of the driving wheel splashers, was surmounted by twin Salter

1 So nicknamed because, despite having steam-blast sanding, they had a habit of slipping at starting if given too heavy a train.

The first Midland Railway 4-2-2 Johnson single, No. 25, built in 1887, with 7 ft 4 in driving wheels, at Bedford.

(Adams Collection, NRM)

MR 4-2-2 Johnson 7 ft 6 in single No. 1853, built in 1889, in photographic grey after construction at Derby. Among the details, note the steam blast pipe joining the sanding pipe in front of the driving wheel.   (*NRM*)

safety valves, the levers above them reaching back to attachments at the tops of two short pillars. This detracted a little from what would otherwise have been perfection of proportion; it was rather as if a beauty queen were sporting a pair of steel-rimmed spectacles. An inverted conical brass cover enclosed additional safety valves on top of the firebox. A handsome chimney, externally tapering slightly upwards and reaching to 13 feet above rail level, crowned the smokebox, whose sides were flush with the boiler. A six-wheeled tender was provided.

Painted in the by now standard MR crimson lake livery, with all the brasswork highly polished, shining metal covers over the outer driving wheel bearings, lining-out in yellow and black, with the number painted on each cab side, the company's coat of arms in the centre of each splasher, and the initial letters 'M' and 'R' placed in the centres of the two tender panels and on the vermilion buffer beams, each engine looked extremely handsome.

Johnson built 18 to this pattern, but after the first eight he put out two that were slightly different from the prototype, with driving wheels two inches wider and an extra half-inch on the cylinder diameters. These were no doubt an experiment, which was evidently considered successful, since in the same year, 1889, a further sequence of 7 ft 6 in engines was begun, and no reversion was made to the smaller diameter subsequently.

In 1893 there were two further changes. The cylinders were widened by another half-inch, and piston valves were fitted in place of slide valves, set beneath the cylinders so that their rods slanted upwards towards the eccentrics on the driving axle. This latter change calls for some comment. Slide valves were the conventional way of admitting steam to the cylinders, cutting it off and then providing an orifice for the exhaust. They had the disadvantage of large flat sliding surfaces which involved, despite oiling, a relatively large amount of friction, so that they wore down relatively rapidly. In a piston valve the rubbing parts had a smaller surface area. However, this type had a defect; if priming occurred and water droplets came over with the steam, these were more likely to penetrate the cylinders than with slide valves, and this could cause damage when a piston reached the end of its stroke, since water might be trapped in the very small space between the piston and the cylinder's end wall and, being incompressible, might force open the end of the cylinder. Walter Smith, the Chief Draughtsman on the North Eastern Railway, designed a piston valve with collapsible segments in the rings, so that if water did get into the valve interior it could escape backwards past the rings; in this way the risk was negated. Johnson's decision to use piston valves of this sort was vindicated when it was found that they wore away only one-sixth as rapidly as slide valves.

In 1896 a further batch of five had the cylinder diameter enlarged by yet another half-inch, the driving wheels at the same time being widened to 7 ft 9 in. More significant, from the point of view of power potential, was the lengthening of the firebox and the increase in the grate area. This was accompanied by a change in boiler

MR 4-2-2 No. 1856, also built in 1889 but with 7 ft 4 in driving wheels and sanding pipes both in front of and behind the driving wheel. The driver is removing char from within the smokebox.
(*Dewhurst Collection, NRM*)

Another fine view of MR No. 1856 outside St Pancras station.
(*Photomatic*)

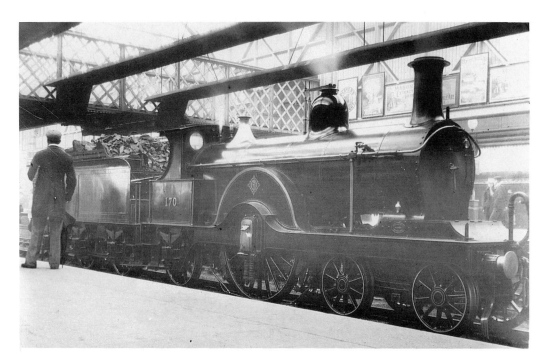

MR 4-2-2 Johnson single
No. 170, with 7 ft 6 in
driving wheels, built in
1893. Note the helical
springs for the driving
wheels, in place of plate
springs. (*Dewhurst Collection NRM*)

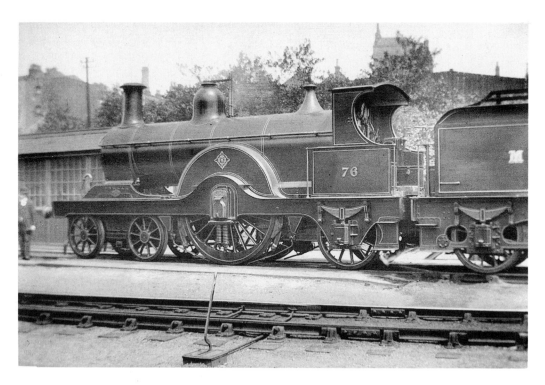

MR 4-2-2 Johnson single
No. 76, of the next
batch, built in 1893, also
with 7 ft 6 in driving
wheels.

type; the larger 'E' class boiler replaced the 'D', and was given an extra 10 lbs per square inch pressure; the frames were slightly lengthened to support it. Ten more similar engines appeared during 1896/7.

Finally, during 1899/1900 the last and largest ten were built. The driving wheels were half an inch wider still, the firebox a foot longer, the boiler, of the 'F' class, was also a foot longer than before and pressed to 180 lbs per square inch. Some of these locomotives were given long double-bogie tenders so that fewer stops for water would be necessary (the MR having as yet laid down no water troughs). When piled high with coal these tenders almost dwarfed the engines they were attached to, and they were in fact a trifle heavier when in working order.

A Midland 'Spinner' was twice exhibited at a Paris exhibition. On the first occasion, in 1889, the newly built

MR Johnson single No. 2601 *Princess of Wales*, with 7 ft 9½ in driving wheels, in superb condition, newly returned from gaining the Grand Prix at the Paris Exhibition of 1899.

(*Photomatic*)

No. 1853 was sent, to be shown alongside Stroudley's 0-4-2 'Gladstone' *Edward Blount* of the LBSCR, and James Stirling's domeless 4-4-0 *Onward* of the South Eastern Railway. It was awarded a gold medal. In 1900 No. 2601, one of the final 7 ft 9½ in batch, was exhibited, together with F. W. Webb's four-cylinder compound *La France* of the LNWR, the NER's six-coupled express engine No. 2006, and Holden's 4-4-0 *Claud Hamilton* of the Great Eastern. Uniquely among MR locomotives,

No. 2601 was given a name, *Princess of Wales*, and stole the show, being awarded the Grand Prix.

These engines, and the later ones especially, although built in such large numbers, had a comparatively short life on main line duties, being gradually superseded by coupled 4-4-0s. The MR had a policy of keeping the weights of its express trains as low as possible, but it could not escape the demands for more comfortable accommodation and better travelling facilities, so loads

MR No. 2601 *Princess of Wales* about to leave St Pancras on the 1.30 pm for Glasgow, September 1901.

(*Ken Nunn Collection, LCGB*)

A MR 4-2-2 single of the final batch, No. 2602, built in 1899, with 7 ft $9\frac{1}{2}$ in driving wheels, in the shed at Kentish Town, London.   (*Photomatic*)

were bound to increase. All the services it provided between London to other provincial cities and to Scotland had to face competition from at least one other line—this was especially the case after the building of the Great Central Railway's London Extension—so it could not afford to skimp, and indeed led the way in the contest for custom, providing not only side-corridor stock, dining saloons with kitchen equipment and sleeping carriages for 1st class passengers, but also for a while, offered the luxury of Pullman class travel on some of its trains.

By about 1900 the writing was on the wall for the single wheeler. The use of the steam sander had given the type a new lease of life, but the Civil Engineer, on the Midland as on all other lines, set a limit which could not be over-ridden. Adhesion weights climbed upwards but might not pass the limit he imposed. So the choice had to be, either coupled driving wheels or double-heading, which latter was uneconomic, for if a train load were only a little more than one single wheeler could manage unaided, to give it another as a pilot was excessive.

✳ ✳ ✳

So the Johnson singles had a comparatively short innings in the railway equivalent of County cricket, especially the later-built ones. They were well liked by their drivers and firemen, despite their tendency to slip

at starting—and in their earlier days, with loads of up to 120 tons, were light on coal. Fortunately their performances have been relatively well recorded during the early 1900s by Charles Rous-Marten, E. L. Ahrons and other worthies of the train-timing fraternity. Most of the logs that were made were taken between St Pancras and Leicester or Nottingham. The engines themselves were shedded at Kentish Town, Leicester, Nottingham and Leeds for the most part, though in 1892 some newly built ones were set to work on the line from Derby to Bristol and shedded at the latter place, or at Birmingham. Unfortunately no one seems to have timed any of these; it would have been interesting to note how they climbed the bank from Bristol through Fishponds and how freely they ran on the level stretches. They would never, of course, have been expected to climb the Lickey Incline unaided; no passenger engine ever did that, banking assistance always being provided.

The main line between St Pancras and Leicester was fortunate in having no steep ascent from its London terminus, but northwards from Hendon there were long stretches of 1 in 176 to 1 in 200, with some much steeper inclines on either side of the intermediate summits of Sharnbrook, Desborough and Kibworth, so that there was plenty of scope for vigorous hill-climbing and fast running on the declivities. On the direct line from Kettering to Nottingham there were also long stretches of moderate steepness, varying between 1 in 142 and 1 in 200. With quite a few enforced slacks en route, neither route was as easy as the GNR main line with which the Stirling singles had to cope, and scheduled average speeds were accordingly a little slower than on the GNR, although as good or better than those demanded on the much easier LNWR main line.

The selection of specimen performances which follows has been made to include the work of as many of the main varieties of Johnson's single wheelers as possible. Charles Rous-Marten, annoyingly failing to furnish exact information about the number of the engine in question, (he merely says it was one of the earliest 7 ft 4 in type) and the load, (which he describes as "12 coaches", presumably the equivalent of twelve six-wheelers) timed a run on the mid-day Manchester express in which over a minute was gained on the schedule between St Pancras and Leicester.

"The first 12½ miles to the Elstree Summit occupied 19 minutes 58 seconds, by no means smart work. The time to St Albans was 28 minutes 9 seconds and to Luton 39 minutes 54 seconds, a distinctly mediocre performance. But then came some much brisker running. Bedford was passed in 16 minutes 57 seconds from Luton, the distance being 19¾ miles, and the maximum rate 80.3 miles an hour. We breasted Sharnbrook Summit in 11 minutes 39 seconds from Bedford, our minimum speed up the 1 in 119 being 33 miles an hour. This was very creditable going. Kettering was passed in 80 minutes 21 seconds from London, the Desborough bank was ascended at a minimum of 38, and our lowest up to Kibworth was 43. Finally we stopped at Leicester in 110 minutes 52 seconds from the start, having averaged 53½ miles an hour."

With a load of about 180 tons this was not bad work at all for a 16-year-old locomotive of this sort, and since time was more than kept the critical remarks seem quite uncalled for. The easy running as far as Luton may have been deliberate, to avoid catching up a preceding train, or simply to let the engine get warmed up. In the same direction Rous-Marten timed one of the same batch of engines (again no number was given) to achieve a better performance with a load some 30 tons heavier than before, on the 2 pm from St Pancras.

"The load ... made itself felt in the climb to Elstree Summit, which was not attained until 19 minutes 2 seconds had elapsed from the London start. St Albans was passed in 27 minutes 13 seconds from St Pancras, and Luton in 38 minutes 26 seconds. Once more a very rapid descent was made down the bank to Bedford, 16 miles of which are at 1 in 200, practically continuous[2], but full speed was attained more slowly than in the other case, so that the 19¾ miles occupied 17 minutes 17 seconds, although a far higher maximum was reached, namely 84.9 miles an hour. Our speed was still as high as 77 when we passed the end of the Bedford platform by the avoiding line. The ascent of the Sharnbrook bank was particularly good, our speed never going below 36 miles an hour and the summit being attained in 11 minutes 39 seconds from Bedford, distance 10 miles. We stopped at Kettering in 80 minutes 21 seconds from London."

2 This is incorrect as only ten miles are inclined at 1 in 200; the other downhill gradients are easier and there are short level and up-hill stretches here and there.

In a sequence of articles about the Johnson singles, published in *The Railway Magazine* during January-March 1910, J. F. Vickery mentions a run behind No. 618—No. 1861 before re-numbering—between Kettering and St Pancras; the load was 222 tons. Station stops were made at Wellingborough, Bedford and Luton, and there were five signal checks, two of which brought the train to a dead stand, at the 62nd milepost and between Leagrave and Luton. The consequence was that 22 minutes were lost through delays, but the engine only lost about 7¾ minutes which included 3¼ minutes standing at signals. The run was recorded in considerable detail, so that it is possible to calculate the approximate speeds attained at different places. A modified version of the log is given, and for an engine now over twenty years old, with a load so much in excess of what it had been designed to haul, this was extremely fine work.

MR 4-2-2 No. 618, Kettering–St Pancras

Miles		Actual time min	sec	Estimated speed
00.0	Kettering	00	00	
02.7	Isham	05	39	
07.0	Wellingborough	09	19	Eased
00.0		00	00	
02.5	Irchester	04	50	
		sig	stop	
08.3	Sharnbrook	18	23	
12.2	Oakley	21	43	72
15.2	Bedford	25	28	
00.0		00	00	
07.9	Ampthill	12	15	
09.5	Flitwick	14	04	50/55
12.5	Harlington	17	29	52
16.9	Leagrave	23	15	
		sig	stop	
19.1	Luton	29	57	
00.0		00	00	
02.9	Chiltern Green	05	31	
05.3	Harpenden	08	17	
10.3	St Albans	12	44	70
15.1	Radlett	16	37	75
17.6	Elstree	19	22	
20.7	Mill Hill	22	34	
23.2	Hendon	24	39	72
		sigs		
28.6	Kentish Town	31	22	
30.2	St Pancras	35	00	

Cecil J. Allen, in the January 1916 issue of *The Railway Magazine*, described a performance he had recorded the previous year by a 7 ft 6 in single with a light load of 100 tons; the engine, No. 642, formerly No. 17, was then 23 years old and being used as a station pilot at Bedford. An 'up' train headed by a 4-4-0, due to pass that station without stopping, halted there because something had gone wrong with the engine. No. 642, together with its driver, was quickly substituted, and

MR 4-2-2 Johnson single No. 123, built in 1898, on an 'up' express passing Radlett.   (*Pilcher Collection, NRM*)

then showed its paces in a remarkable way. The uphill gradient, steepening after Elstow to 1 in 200, was tackled without speed falling below $52\frac{3}{4}$ at Ampthill. The $1\frac{1}{2}$ easier miles to Flitwick allowed it to rise to $62\frac{1}{2}$, on the second 1 in 200 stretch to milepost 34 it had settled down to a steady 55, and $64\frac{1}{4}$ was then reached at Leagrave before the Luton stop. After the re-start the rate rose quickly; St Albans was passed at $71\frac{1}{2}$, the maximum in the dip just before Radlett was over 80, the minimum at Elstree was $64\frac{1}{4}$, and $77\frac{1}{2}$ was attained at Hendon. St Pancras was reached in almost $6\frac{1}{2}$ minutes under schedule. This run by an old-timer with an old-time loading demonstrated what it no doubt often achieved in its youth when there was no-one present to record its feats, and shows that the 'Spinners', like the Stirling 8-footers, could climb well when put to it. The relevant part of Allen's log is as follows:

Miles		min	sec
00.0	Bedford	00	00
07.9	Ampthill	10	15
12.4	Harlington	14	50
16.9	Leagrave	19	45
19.6	Luton	22	25
00.0		00	00
02.9	Chiltern Green	05	15
05.5	Harpenden	07	55
10.3	St Albans	12	15
15.1	Radlett	15	50
17.6	Elstree	18	20
20.7	Mill Hill	21	00
23.2	Hendon	22	55
28.6	Kentish Town	28	00
30.2	St Pancras	30	35

Coming now to the 7 ft 9 in engines with $19\frac{1}{2}$-inch cylinders with piston valves, built during 1896/7, Vickery records a series of test runs with No. 115 which showed how economically they ran. The locomotive was tested during a five-day period over the St Pancras–Nottingham route, going one way each day in either direction. Total loads, including the weights of engine and tender, varied between 170 and 240 tons. Weather conditions were 'fine and dry' on the first two days; winds of varying strength prevailed on the other three. In all 1,240 miles were run; the total amount of coal burnt was 13.6 tons, which averaged out at 24.56 lbs per mile and 2.88 lbs per indicated HP per hour. For each pound of coal burned 9.33 lbs of water (a little under a gallon) was consumed. On every run the mean average speed was greater than the booked speed. The tests were carried out soon after the locomotive had been constructed and the results were regarded as very satisfactory.

In *The Engineer* for 24 June 1904 Rous-Marten mentioned a recent run he had had behind No. 117, a sister engine of No. 115 whose tests have just been referred to. He is skimpy on details, but at least mentions speeds attained:

"No. 117 . . . the actual engine, by the way, that first achieved the honour of authentically reaching 90 mph, was on the 12 noon Manchester fast express from London to Leicester. The load behind the tender was 160 tons, and the running time from start to stop was 107 min 8 sec with a permanent way slack near Kettering. No exceptional

downhill speeds were run in this instance, the highest being 77.5 mph which was reached at three different points. The lowest up-grade rates were 34.6 up Sharnbrook, 40.6 up Desborough and 42.8 up Kibworth. Bedford was passed in 52 min 13 sec from the St Pancras start."

More notice was taken of the performances of the last ten engines built during 1899/1900, which had larger boilers, fireboxes and tenders and fractionally larger driving wheels. Of these, No. 2601 *Princess of Wales* was the best known and probably the most photographed. Vickery mentions a run timed by Rous-Marten, with a load of '15 coaches' (probably 170–180 tons), when this locomotive gained 7 min 10 sec on the 230-minute schedule of the 'up' Scotch express from Leeds to St Pancras, in spite of seven signal and permanent way delays and overtime spent at Trent Junction. Unfortunately Rous-Marten was, as so often, short with information about what must have been an exceptionally good run. The Trent Junction–St Pancras part of the journey was covered in seven minutes less than schedule, Leicester (20.5 miles) being passed in 24 minutes, Kettering (47.6 miles) in 55 min 40 sec, Bedford (69.8 miles) in 75 min 50 sec, Luton (89.4 miles) in 96 min 21 sec and St Albans (99.7 miles) in 108 min 53 sec. St Pancras was reached in 128 minutes exactly. From these times one can assume that if any of the reported checks occurred on this part of the journey, they would have been

MR Johnson single No. 688 (originally No. 2605) on an 'up' express near Welsh Harp. Note the altered smokebox with numberplate, the consequence of re-modelling by Deeley. (*Laundy Collection, NRM*)

between Luton and St Albans. In the opposite direction the same recorder timed a sister engine, hauling 140 tons, to reach Leicester three minutes early from St Pancras, despite signal delays and other checks, in a net time of $99\frac{1}{2}$ minutes. This, too, was clearly a very fine run.

Rous-Marten also timed a sister engine of *Princess of Wales*, hauling 170 tons, on a London-bound train from Leicester which passed Bedford only one minute outside even time, despite having to climb the Kibworth, Desborough and Sharnbrook summits en route and having to slacken speed over the recently laid water troughs at Oakley. About this part of the journey he is maddeningly uninformative, giving only the minima at Desborough and Sharnbrook summits (38 and 40.6 mph respectively) and no passing times until Bedford ($49\frac{1}{4}$ miles in 50 min 17 sec from Leicester.) After that, to his chagrin, the quality of the run deteriorated, with a minimum before Leagrave of only 39.1 mph at the top of the 1 in 200. Signal checks spoiled the conclusion of the run, which nevertheless reached St Pancras in one second under 112 minutes. Quite possibly the slow running after Bedford was due to the driver being aware that there was a train in front of him, and running that according to Rous-Marten was 'relatively poor' was in fact thoroughly sensible.

During their working lives the Johnson singles underwent little change through rebuilding. After R. M. Deeley had succeeded Johnson as Locomotive Superintendent at the beginning of 1904, all the company's stock of engines were re-numbered, and the 4-2-2s were given numbers in the order in which they had been built, between 600 and 694. Such alterations as some of them received were cosmetic rather than structural. Most

Midland Railway 4-2-2s, 1887–1900

Years of construction	No. built	Numbers given	Weight of locomotive in working order (tons)	Adhesion weight (tons)	Total wheelbase (ft in)	Driving wheel diameter (ft in)	Cylinder diameter × stroke (in)	Boiler type†	Boiler pressure (lbs per sq in)	Length of firebox (ft)	Grate area (sq ft)	Tractive effort at 85% of working pressure (lbs)
1887/8	8	25–29 30–32	43.5	18	21 9½	7 4	18 × 26	D	160	6½	19.6	13,018
1889	2	34 1853	43.5	18.5	21 9½	7 6	18½ × 26	D	160	6½	19.6	13,752
1889/90	10	37 1854–1857 1858–1862	43.5	18	21 9½	7 4	18 × 26	D	160	6½	19.6	13,018
1889/90	5	1863–1867	43.5	18.5	21 9½	7 6	18½ × 26	D	160	6½	19.6	13,752
1891/3	35	4, 8, 16, 17, 20, 24, 33, 35, 36, 38, 39, 94–97, 100, 122, 129, 133, 145, 149, 170–178, 1868–1872	44.15	18.5	21 9½	7 6*	18½ × 26	D	160	6½	19.6	13,752
1893/6	10	75–77 79, 88 179, 183	44.5	18.5	21 9½	7 6*	19 × 26**	D	160	6½	19.6	14,183
1896/9	15	115–121 123–128 130, 131	47.12	18.5	21 11½	7 9*	19½ × 26**	E	170	7	21.3	15,361
1899/1900	10	19–23 2601–2605	50.2	18.8	22 11½	7 9½*	19½ × 26**	F	180	8	24.5	16,177

*With twin spiral springs in place of plate springs.
**With piston valves instead of slide valves.
†Total heating surfaces of boilers: D—1,240.6 sq ft; E—1,233 sq ft; F—1,217 sq ft.
(The decrease in boiler heating surface was more than made up for by the increase in firebox heating surface.)

received a slightly different pattern of chimney and a Deeley-type smokebox door. More noticeable was the simplified style of painting, with less lining-out. The initials 'MR' disappeared from the tenders and were replaced by the locomotive's number in large gold figures. On the engines themselves the numbers were removed from the cab sides and a small number-plate with white figures on a black background was placed on the upper part of the smokebox door. The company's coat of arms also disappeared from the driving wheel splashers.

Once the new 4-4-0 three-cylinder compounds began to emerge from Derby Works, the single wheelers were gradually taken off main line duties, and ended their days on minor assignments, such as being held in reserve as station pilots or running light trains on such easily graded lines as the one between Nottingham and Lincoln. Some also worked as pilots to other engines on heavy trains. During the First World War, when there were locomotive shortages, some even found themselves piloting freight engines on heavy coal trains.

Withdrawals began in 1919, and by 1928 there were no more to be seen. One, however, No. 118, of the 1896/7 batch, with 7 ft 9 in wheels and piston valves, was set aside for preservation, restored to its original appearance and put on exhibition at Derby Works, where it remained for 35 years before being transferred to Leicester Museum of Transport. It is now in the National Railway Museum, York.

Midland 'Spinner' No. 118 in the course of restoration for preservation at Derby Works in 1931.   (*Photomatic*)

6 The Caledonian Showpiece

In 1886 an international exhibition was held in Edinburgh and Messrs Neilson & Co., the Glasgow firm of engineers determined to build an engine for exhibition there, and for subsequent sale to the Caledonian Railway. (They had already constructed many locomotives to the designs of Dugald Drummond while he was Locomotive Superintendent, first on the North British and then on the CR.)

It is not clear who first propounded the idea of a single wheeler. On the face of it, it was an unsuitable choice for a Scottish railway whose main lines between Carlisle and Glasgow, Edinburgh and Aberdeen included a number of steeply-graded inclines, notably the southern approach to Beattock Summit, with its long stretches of 1 in 74 to 1 in 88. Other lines south of the Border had all confined their single wheelers, and were to continue to confine them, to routes that either had no steep banks or, if there were any, to stretches where the banks were short.

It might have been supposed that Neilson could have built one of Drummond's highly successful 66 class of express 4-4-0s, of which they had already constructed ten, and which were coping with the mainline trains from the south to the two chief Scottish cities with great success. However, Dübs & Co., their fellow engineers in Glasgow, were about to build one of these, also for

showing at the Edinburgh International Exhibition, so the choice had to be of something distinguishably different. The reflowering of the bogie single wheeler was about to begin, and S. W. Johnson's experiments on the Midland with engines which had had their coupling rods removed were no doubt known within the engineering fraternity. Perhaps Neilson wished to get in first with a new idea, making the point that here was the express locomotive of the future. Certainly this would increase the attention paid to it at the Exhibition.

However, if this were so it seems strange that the first sketch was for an outside-cylindered engine with driving wheels as much as 8 ft 3 in across, though otherwise resembling a Drummond engine in shape and style. Single driving wheels of such a size had seldom been used before; the only precedent was the fitting of 8 ft 6 in wheels to the London & North Western engine *Cornwall* (as mentioned in Chapter 1) and a few locomotives with 8 ft 10 in wheels on the Bristol & Exeter Railway, which the Great Western rebuilt as 8-footers as soon as they could lay their hands on them.

Sketch of a possible single wheeler for the Caledonian Railway, with outside cylinders and 8 ft 3 in driving wheels, submitted by Neilson & Co., but rejected in favour of one with smaller wheels and inside cylinders.

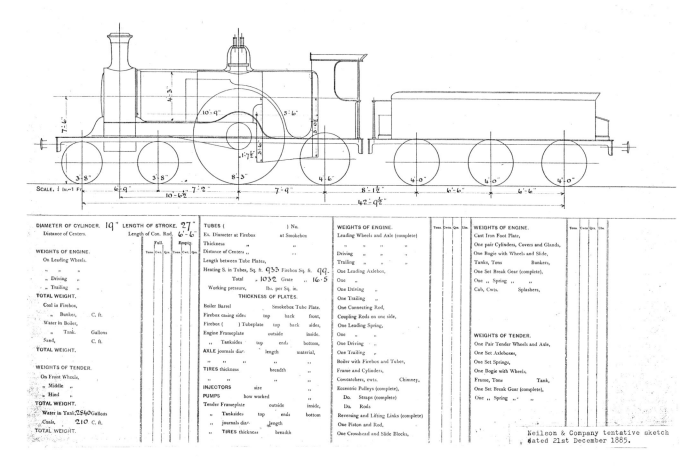

Neilson & Company tentative sketch dated 21st December 1885.

Perhaps Stirling's 8-footers were the inspiration, along with his notion that large wheels gripped the rails better. However, the sketch merely remained the record of a proposal that was not followed up. The new engine's design was probably the product of the collective wisdom of Neilson's drawing office, whose Chief Draughtsman later declared in a magazine article that Drummond himself never intervened in the drawing out of the design of the engine that *was* built. Drummond was not the man to fail to challenge that statement if it were not correct. Yet it remains true that in all visible respects except the lack of coupled wheels it did appear to be a Drummond engine. So it seems likely that Drummond was consulted, turned down the first idea, agreed to the second and after that occasionally gave advice when asked. At the end of 1885 the CR Board agreed to purchase the engine after it had been shown at the Edinburgh Exhibition, for a cost of £2,600. Unsuitable though the design might be for the railway's needs, it would none the less make a splendid advertisement for the company when exhibited in its blue livery.

The CR's offer was not actually made to Neilson for three weeks, by which time a more acceptable design had been selected. The cylinders were to be inside the frames and the driving wheel diameter was reduced to 7 feet. Now followed a race against time, as the engine had to be delivered at the Exhibition by 1st April 1886; there were barely nine weeks in which to construct it. It was helpful that many of the components were the same as those of the 66 class 4-4-0s which had been built before. But there were also some innovations. The boiler had to be pitched 3 inches higher to clear the single driving axle and its cranks, and was a little over 2 inches narrower; the firebox was also somewhat shorter and there were 30 fewer firetubes. The dome, directly above the line of the driving axle, was surmounted, as in all Drummond engines, by two Ramsbottom safety valves. The sand blast to the driving wheel rims was as F. C. Holt, its MR designer, had originally intended, the pressure coming from air in the Westinghouse reservoir. The Westinghouse Company does not seem to have raised any objection, as it did in the case of the experimental MR engines; either it did not know or did not bother when it did know, possibly deciding that it did not really matter after all, as sand would be used when the locomotive was trying to move, not when it had to be brought to a halt, and there would be some interval between such occasions during which the pressure could be restored.

The chief innovation was the employment of the

Cross-sectional diagrams of No. 123 showing, among other things, the steam-jacketing of the cylinders, the annular blast pipe and the compressed air sanding gear.

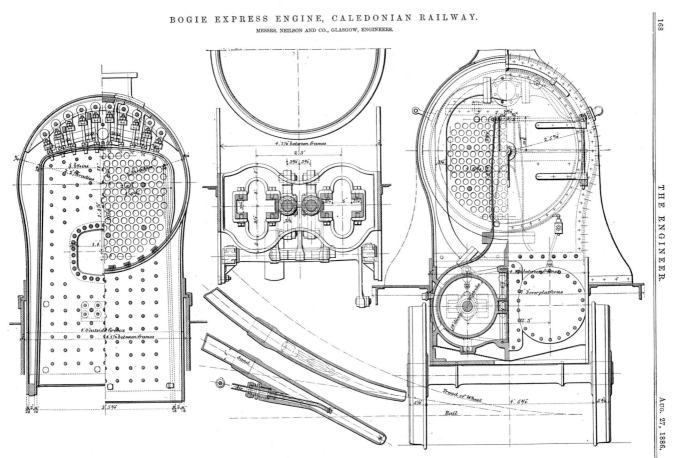

BOGIE EXPRESS ENGINE, CALEDONIAN RAILWAY.

MESSRS. NEILSON AND CO., GLASGOW, ENGINEERS.

168

THE ENGINEER.

AUG. 27, 1886.

vortex blast pipe, first used on the London & South Western Railway by W. Adams, the Locomotive Superintendent whom Drummond was later to succeed. In this the blast from the exhaust steam was driven upwards through an orifice of annular section towards the base of the chimney; within this ring was a pipe whose lower end curved back and widened out to face the lower tubes of the boiler where they entered the smokebox. This gave the exhaust jet a greater sucking power to exercise on the gases from the firebox, and so improved the draught. Another innovation was the double whistle which projected from the top of the outer firebox as two side-by-side tubes, a louder one for use when the locomotive was in action hauling a train and a quieter one for when it was moving on its own in station and goods yards. A decorative feature, which Drummond's other engines had not carried, was a continuous wheel splasher across the tops of the bogie wheels on either side, similar to those on the GNR 8-footers. The tender had outside frames with the upper edges of the slots being upwardly curved, and four sets of steps, one on each side at either end. Behind the tender tank, just in front of the rear

buffer beams, there was a long tool-box with a hinged lid.

Special attention was paid to the engine's appearance. The axle ends, chimney cap and cab fittings were brightly polished, and the lining out was in black and white against the usual bright blue livery. The CR coat of arms appeared on the centre of the tender sides but the railway's initial letters themselves were omitted. The builder's numberplate appeared prominently on each splasher, and on each cab side another oval plate showed the number 123 bracketed between the words 'CALEDONIAN RAILWAY' curved above and below.

When completed the locomotive made a most impressive showpiece. It duly arrived at the Exhibition on time and remained there until it closed at the end of December, where it vied for public admiration with the equally gorgeous Drummond-designed CR 4-4-0 No. 124, built by Dübs & Co, which was generally similar to the 66 class engines. In the New Year both engines were transferred to the CR main line, and No. 123 worked expresses daily from Edinburgh Princes Street to Carlisle and back. Some years later it was removed from that

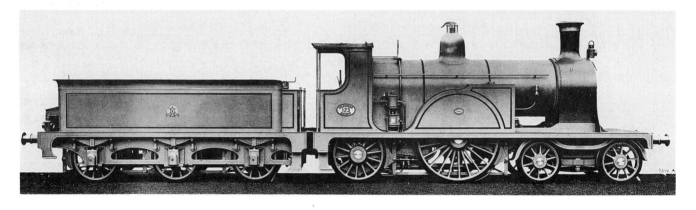

4-2-2 No. 123 in Caledonian light blue livery, as built by Neilson & Co. in 1886 and exhibited at the Edinburgh Exhibition.

A closer view of CR No. 123. Note the two whistles above the firebox.

duty to work trains between Perth and Aberdeen, and was also occasionally used as a pilot engine for the Royal Train during the last years of Queen Victoria's reign—not an onerous duty in view of the upper limit of 40 mph for all railway journeys which Her Majesty undertook. Eventually it was commandeered to head the Directors' Saloon. In 1905 it was given a new boiler by Drummond's successor, J. McIntosh, with a slightly higher boiler pressure. In 1914 it was re-numbered 1123 on the 'duplicate list'. Then in 1923 it passed into LMS ownership.

There was still plenty of life left in No. 123—or No. 14010 as it now became—but for a while the former chromatic splendour vanished; the LMS crimson lake livery replaced the former bright blue, and the new number appeared in large figures on the tender sides. All the little touches of brilliance disappeared. The distinctive dome-top safety valves had already disappeared with the first re-boilering, a new pair being fitted on the firebox top with the whistle being shifted back to make room for it. In 1924 yet another boiler was fitted. In this form No. 14010 ran for some years on light trains between Perth and Dundee, an almost level line, and eventually clocked a total of 780,000 miles before it was decided to withdraw it from regular service in 1935. To its credit, the LMS management then determined that in view of its distinguished early history, recounted below, it ought to be preserved. It was restored to its former livery (although, because it had been twice rebuilt, not to its former appearance), was re-married to its original tender and kept for a while as a museum piece. In 1958 British Railways agreed to take the locomotive out of retirement and restore it to full working order. Initially,

Caledonian Railway 4-2-2 No. 123

Date ordered:	23rd January 1886
Date delivered:	1st April 1886*
Builders:	Neilson & Co.
Boiler – length:	10 ft 7 in
width:	4 ft 3 in
heating surface:	950.1 sq ft
	(980.1 sq ft when rebuilt)
Firebox heating surface:	103 sq ft
Grate area:	17.5 sq ft
Boiler pressure:	150 lbs per sq in
	(160 lbs per sq in when rebuilt)
Cylinders:	18 in × 26 in**
Wheels – bogie:	3 ft 6 in
driving:	7 ft
trailing:	4 ft 6 in
Total wheelbase:	21 ft 1 in
Weight of engine in working order:	41 tons 17 cwt 1 qr
Adhesion weight:	17 tons
Tractive effort at 85% working pressure:	12,790 lbs
Tender – coal:	4½ tons
water:	2,850 galls
Weight of tender in working order:	33 tons 9 cwt

*Delivery date to Edinburgh Exhibition. The CR took delivery on 1st January 1887.
**Steam-jacketed.

CR 4-2-2 No. 123 in 1920, after its first re-boilering by McIntosh, and with a different tender.

(Ken Nunn Collection, LCGB)

CR 4-2-2 No. 123 in LMS livery and re-numbered 14010 after its second re-boilering; note the disappearance of the safety valve from the top of the dome.   (*Photomatic*)

it worked a number of special trains in connection with the Scottish Industries Fair of 1959 but was later used on chartered railway enthusiasts' trains. It was often attached to a pair of old Caledonian Railway carriages, also restored in their former CR livery. On some trips it travelled far from its original haunts, getting to places such as Oban and Stranraer, where it had never been seen before, working over gradients fiercer even than those on the Beattock road.

In 1963 the restored No. 123 made its most remarkable journey when it travelled south to work "The Blue Belle" on 15th September. This train ran from London, Victoria, working through to Horsted Keynes, Sussex, on the Bluebell Railway, double-heading with LSWR T9 class 4-4-0 No. 120, the locomotives being serviced at Brighton before their return to London.

No. 123 was finally retired in 1965 and now has pride

The 'Caley single' as No. 14010 leaving Perth with a train for Dundee.   (*Nevitt Collection, NRM*)

No. 123 as restored to its original livery and re-united with its original tender. (*Mitchell Library, Glasgow*)

No. 123 with its special two-coach train pre-served and re-painted in Caledonian Railway livery, leaving Glasgow, St Enoch. (*Mitchell Library, Glasgow*)

Flanked by a Stanier "Black Five", No. 123 is about to leave
St Enoch station with the special train.

(Mitchell Library, Glasgow)

of place in the Glasgow Museum of Transport at Kelvin
Hall, Glasgow, where it is preserved along with several
other historic Scottish locomotives and tramcars.

* * *

The 'Caley Single' does not seem to have engaged the
attentions of train-timers enough to have left records of
its abilities in print, except during one memorable month
when it carved for itself a niche in railway history soon
after its construction, during the 'Race to Edinburgh' of
August 1888. This event arose from the desire of the
West Coast route authorities to draw level with those of
the East Coast route in the contest for passenger custom.
Until 1887 the rival companies were content to ignore
each other, one offering a faster, the other a more
comfortable, journey. The 10 am from Euston had a
portion for Edinburgh which was reached in a leisurely
ten hours, while the corresponding day train from King's
Cross, the "Flying Scotsman", which also left at 10 am,

required only nine hours, despite having to wait at York
for a luncheon interval of half an hour (the corresponding interval for the West Coast train being 20 minutes at
Preston). However, the East Coast train did not convey
3rd class passengers, while the West Coast one did.

Then, in November 1887, 3rd class coaches were for
the first time included in the "Flying Scotsman" for the
benefit of persons going the whole way to Edinburgh,
and at once the advantage shifted to King's Cross; 3rd
class passengers now began to forsake the West Coast
route for its rival. The wish now arose among West
Coast officials for some counter-stroke to be made,
despite the objections of the London & North Western's
Chairman, Richard Moon, who thought that comfort,
convenience and punctuality mattered everything, and
speed hardly at all when it came to attracting passengers.
It certainly could not be denied that the West Coast
coaching stock was more comfortable and smoother
riding than that used on the East Coast route, which a
contemporary wag once accused of having octagonal
wheels.

From June 1888 a process began by which the West
Coast authorities accelerated their 10 am train at short
notice, the other side promptly responding in the same

manner, until at the commencement of the first full week in August a general race was in progress—a kind of relay race between teams of locomotives in which the baton to be handed over was a rake of passenger coaches. Details of the Race do not matter here; what is relevant is the part CR No. 123 took on the final stage of the West Coast journey, the 100.6 miles from Carlisle to Princes Street, Edinburgh. No. 123 was used to head the Edinburgh portion each weekday between 6th and 31st August and had the task of hauling four short bogie coaches, with a tare weight of 80 tons, on a 112-minute booking. The scheduled time was cut on every single occasion, and most of the arrivals at Princes Street were from two to four minutes early, but during the first week the pace was hotter, with an 8-minute gain on the Monday and Tuesday and a 7-minute gain on the Wednesday. On the following day the racing train arrived late from the south because of an engine failure at Shap, so there was an incentive to make up time, and the gain on this occasion (though the train still arrived late) was as much as $9\frac{1}{2}$ minutes. This record of $102\frac{1}{2}$ minutes stood for a long while as the fastest run between Carlisle and Edinburgh.

This particular journey naturally provoked great in-

The chart of No. 123's record performance between Carlisle and Edinburgh, Princes Street on 9th August 1888, with a train of 80 tons.   (*The Engineer*)

terest, and Dugald Drummond was obliging enough to send to *The Engineer* for publication a chart in which the speeds attained, mile by mile, were shown in the form of a graph which matched a gradient profile. (Clearly some official—it could hardly have been the guard—was on board with a stopwatch.) There seems little point in describing the run verbally, since a copy of Drummond's chart is reproduced here. But one may note the rapid start from Carlisle, 71 mph being attained beyond Floriston in less than eight miles—the short 1 in 110 downhill from Carlisle platform would have been of material assistance here, especially to a single wheeler— and the high minimum speeds at the tops of the two subsequent 1 in 200 inclines. A second 71 mph was attained near Nethercleugh, and Beattock bank itself, after ten miles at 1 in 88/75, was surmounted at what must then have been a record minimum of $36\frac{1}{2}$ mph; later Cobbinshaw summit was passed, after three miles at 1 in 132/173/100, at $54\frac{1}{2}$—again probably a record. However, no high speeds were attempted on the descents, $73\frac{1}{2}$ mph being the maximum beyond Cobbinshaw, and the serrations in the graph suggest that the brakes were applied several times. Finally one notes the very rapid stop made at the end of the journey, from 65 mph to the dead stand in Princes Street in a single mile—something typical of Caledonian express running and showing the trust drivers had in their Westinghouse brakes. In his book *The Railway Race to the North*, O. S. Nock included a

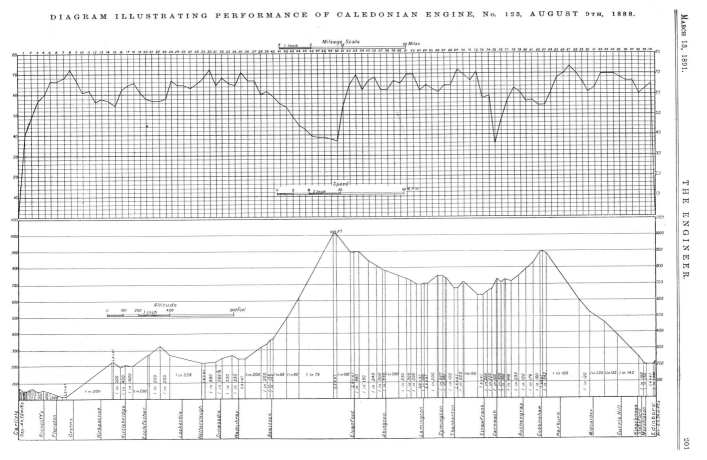

DIAGRAM ILLUSTRATING PERFORMANCE OF CALEDONIAN ENGINE, No. 123, AUGUST 9TH, 1888.

MARCH 13, 1891.

THE ENGINEER.

201

detailed log of the journey which is reproduced here, compiled from the detail given in the chart.

Caledonian Railway 4-2-2 No. 123, Carlisle–Edinburgh, 9th August 1888

Load: 4 coaches 80 tons

Miles		Actual time min	sec	Speed (mph)
00.0	Carlisle	00	00	
04.1	Rockcliffe	05	35	
08.6	Gretna	09	38	72 max
13.1	Kirkpatrick	14	07	
16.7	Kirtlebridge	17	46	54½ min
20.1	Ecclefechan	21	04	65½ max
25.8	Lockerbie	26	46	57 min
28.7	Nethercleugh	29	22	
31.7	Dinwoodie	31	54	72 max
34.5	Wamphray	34	26	64½ min
39.7	Beattock	39	13	71 max
42.0	Mp 42	41	44	52
44.0	Mp 44	44	20	43
46.0	Mp 46	47	17	39
48.0	Mp 48	50	23	38½
49.7	Beattock Summit	53	04	36½ min
52.6	Elvanfoot	56	05	
55.3	Crawford	58	42	69½ max
57.8	Abington	60	52	

Miles		Actual time min	sec	Speed (mph)
63.2	Lamington	65	35	
66.9	Symington	69	04	
68.5	Thankerton	70	29	72 max
70.0	Leggatfoot	71	45	65 min
72.0	Mp 72	73	28	72 max
73.2	Strawfrank Junction	74	44	
74.8	Carnwath	77	16	63 max
79.1	Auchengray	81	55	
82.2	Cobbinshaw	85	13	54½ min
85.3	Harburn	88	16	73½ max
89.3	Midcalder Junction	91	45	
95.1	Currie Hill	96	58	
98.4	Slateford	99	58	
100.0	Mp 100	101	28	65
100.6	Edinburgh (Princes Street)	102	33	

This was No. 123's short span of glory. No sooner had the 'Race to Edinburgh' ended than train loads began to increase. In the similar 'Race to Aberdeen' which took place seven years later, no single wheelers were used at all on the West Coast route, the honours being carried off by 4-4-0s of Drummond's 66 class between Carlisle and Perth, and of his successor Lambie's design from there to Aberdeen. By then No. 123 had been assigned to less exacting duties.

7 The North Eastern Two-Cylinder Compounds

The North Eastern Railway built its last 2-2-2 single wheeler in 1866, the final example of Edward Fletcher's 950 class, the first of which had been built in 1861. From then onwards, for 22 years, only coupled locomotives were built, though the NER system was more suitable than many for single wheelers, having long level, or nearly level stretches, especially in Yorkshire. For many years Anglo-Scottish expresses on the East Coast route, invariably hauled south of York by Stirling single wheelers, had 2-4-0s substituted for the latter for the rest of their journey northwards.

During most of this period Fletcher was Locomotive Superintendent at Gateshead (where the NER locomotives were mostly built until the move to Darlington early the following century), and under his leadership all the locomotives produced for passenger work were four-coupled. On his retirement in 1883 Alexander McDonnell, from the Great Southern & Western Railway of Ireland, succeeded him, and found himself facing something like a chaos of old-fashioned engines of all shapes and sizes—and facing, too, the determined opposition of many of the NER enginemen whose viewpoints, however radical they might be politically, were thoroughly conservative when it came to upholding established practices. After a year and a half of tilting vainly at obstreperous windmills, he resigned in disgust, and for a long while the NER had no Locomotive Superintendent, the Board waiting for the storm to die down.

Then, in 1885, Thomas W. Worsdell was appointed to the vacancy. He came from Stratford Works, on the Great Eastern Railway, where he had been Locomotive Superintendent for four years, leaving a good post for a better one, since the NER was the most profitable line in the United Kingdom and ranked in importance with the Midland and the Great Northern despite having no headquarters in the capital. His brother, Wilson Worsdell, was already in a senior position at Gateshead, and was later to succeed him.

T. W. Worsdell had railways in his blood. He was the eldest son of Nathaniel Worsdell, who had been Carriage Superintendent on the Grand Junction Railway until it merged with other lines to form the London & North Western, and who with his own father had helped to build the tender of Stephenson's *Rocket*. In his youth Thomas spent some time at Crewe before going to the United States to work for the Pennsylvania Railroad, where his abilities very soon earned him a position of high responsibility. Francis Webb, on the LNWR, had his eye on him, and when Webb succeeded Ramsbottom as Locomotive Superintendent on that railway he invited Worsdell back to be his Works Manager. In this position the latter remained for ten years, being involved not only in the building of the highly successful 'Precedent' class 2-4-0s, but also of the earliest of Webb's ill-starred three-cylinder compounds. His stay at Crewe appears to have left him favouring the principle of compounding, but he also saw that Webb's system was unsatisfactory, and after he went to Stratford he tried a new method which had appeared to work well in Germany.

Herr von Borries, Chief Mechanical Engineer on the Hanover State Railway, built some experimental 2-4-0s for passenger trains, each of which had one high-pressure and one low-pressure cylinder, both external to the frames and linked by an intermediate steam receiver. As to their appearance, the less said the better, but they seem to have satisfied their designer; the idea behind them was elegant even if they themselves were not. One larger low-pressure cylinder took over the exhausted steam from the high-pressure one, and both were so proportioned that each gave approximately the same thrust. Von Borries had to face one difficulty: when the engine was expected to start, if the piston in the high-pressure cylinder happened to be at one end or the other of its stroke it could not apply any leverage to its crank, and the other cylinder's piston could not do so either since it had not yet received any steam. To counter this he fixed a special valve to a spindle in the pipe between the receiver and the low-pressure cylinder which would allow steam to enter the latter directly from the boiler, so that for a few turns of the wheels the locomotive functioned as a two-cylinder simple. Once the receiver was full of steam given up from the smaller cylinder, its pressure closed the valve and full compounding began.

While on the GER Worsdell had built a number of engines on this principle, using an automatic valve to permit both cylinders to receive boiler steam when starting, as von Borries had done, though it was a flap valve of simpler construction. He also enclosed both cylinders within the frames, thus concealing from the eye the fact that they were of different diameters, and substituted for the German engine's box-shaped receiver a wide pipe which curved around the inner top of the smokebox. The only way to recognize them when they were in action was to listen to their exhausts—two for each revolution of the wheels instead of four—once they had got going. After some re-designing of the automatic valve the system functioned satisfactorily, and tests appeared to show that these engines were rather lighter on coal than non-compounds of similar sizes and dimensions doing the same work. However, they had their faults; they could pull well enough at low speeds but would not run freely when required to go faster.

None the less, Worsdell thought the method was worth perpetuating, and soon after moving to Gateshead in 1885 he began to construct two-cylinder compounds for the NER—first 0-6-0 freight engines, then 0-6-2 tanks, then a solitary 2-4-0 passenger locomotive, and then, modelled on the latter, some 4-4-0 passenger express engines. One of these, No. 117, performed with distinction in the 1888 'Race to Edinburgh' by covering the 124.4 miles from Newcastle to Edinburgh Waverley in 126 minutes, the fastest time so far made.

Then, to everyone's surprise, he proceeded to construct some bogie single wheelers, all two-cylinder compounds. They were to be his last achievements, for in

1890 his health began to fail and he retired, his younger brother Wilson Worsdell succeeding him. The latter, having no special attachment to compounding, altered his brother's engines one by one to simple expansion working, and within a few years the two-cylinder compound type was confined to freight engines.

To fly in the face of North Eastern tradition and bring back the single wheeler needs some explaining, but reasons may be advanced. By the end of 1888 the bogie single had become very much *à la mode*. Three main line railways, the Midland in particular, had begun to employ the type for their fast trains. There had always been a close sympathy between Derby and Gateshead, which was especially to be seen later when a type of 4-4-0 three-cylinder compound designed by the NER's Chief Draughtsman, W. M. Smith, was adopted by Johnson in his last years on the MR, and was continued, with slight modifications, by his successor; hence the famous 'Midland Compounds'.

By the summer of 1888 the first of the MR's 'Spinners' were running from St Pancras, and the CR's No. 123 was showing its paces between Carlisle and Edinburgh. The NER, as already noted, had routes far more suitable for single wheelers than the MR or CR main lines, on which adhesion was not likely to present problems when steam sanding was available, and rails of heavier section and tougher steel allowed the driving wheels to take more weight. The single, too, cost less to build and had fewer moving parts. If it were a case of horses for courses, the NER had the courses for this sort of horse.

It cannot be said that Worsdell plunged rashly into

North Eastern Railway 4-2-2 two-cylinder compound No. 1326 of Class I, with 7 ft 1 in driving wheels, in photographic grey, immediately after construction at Gateshead Works. (*NRM*)

building 4-2-2s, for he only constructed ten of his first type, the I class, the first two of which emerged from Gateshead at the end of 1888. Like the CR's No. 123 they had 7-foot wheels; like the 'Spinners' they were sanded by steam, not compressed air; unlike the 'Spinners' the frames were inside the wheels; unlike both the other types and the Irish engines they each had a commodious cab of the sort which was to characterize NER locomotives from T. W. Worsdell's day onwards. Most distinctively of all, the front end was, among single wheelers, unique. The Worsdell-von Borries two-cylinder compound system was used. Worsdell placed one 18-inch high-pressure cylinder alongside one 26-inch low-pressure cylinder, using, as in his other compound engines, a long curved pipe as an intermediate steam receiver to connect the two. It proved just possible to get the cylinder block between the front ends of the frames, by dint of cutting a hole in one of the latter so that the larger cylinder could bulge out through it.

However, there was no room for the cylinder valves in what had become the usual place with inside-cylindered engines, that is between the cylinders, so they had to be set above them. To operate them Worsdell fitted Joy's valve gear. This type of gear, which was used on the LNWR as long as that company had an independent existence, and which also became standard on the Lancashire & Yorkshire Railway, had certain advantages but one drawback, the fact that the connecting rod was weakened by having to be drilled through, which was not very important until engines grew larger and steam pressures increased to put strain on the point of weakness.

In the Joy gear the movement of each valve was operated from a point along the connecting rod, where a pin passed through it within a bush. The movement of this pin, in a lateral ellipse as the rod moved forwards

and backwards, actuated the movement of the slide valve. The reversing mechanism in the cab moved a radius rod attached to the valve spindle up or down within a slotted guide bar pivoted at its mid-point, whose ends vibrated to and fro by levers attached to the connecting rod pin. It was an elegant method of achieving the desired end, and required much less weight of metal, and in particular of moving metal, than did other valve gears which were operated from eccentrics on the driving axle, whose large rubbing surfaces also used up much oil. Worsdell had been familiar with the Joy gear on the LNWR and preferred it. In the finished engine the difference in the valve gear would hardly have been noticed by the casual observer.

In 1890 the 7-foot singles were followed by a further ten of the J class, somewhat larger and intended for the main line expresses between York and Edinburgh. The Forth Bridge was about to be opened, and the anticipated extra traffic beyond Edinburgh suggested that trains south of that city might also increase in weight. One would have supposed that Worsdell would have built a larger version of his previous compound 4-4-0 instead of a new 4-2-2; this must surely be the only occasion of a single wheeler type being constructed to replace a four-coupled type in *expectation* of heavier trains. In the new engine the driving wheels were increased in diameter to 7 ft 7 in and each of the two cylinders was made 2 inches wider, the stroke being the same at 24 inches. Placing the two differently sized cylinders side by side in the I class single had been a tight fit, only made possible by cutting the hole in the right-hand frame, but in the J class it simply could not be done, so the very unusual expedient was adopted of

placing the smaller high-pressure cylinder below, and the larger low-pressure one above, the horizontal plane of the driving axle, towards which the piston rods were appropriately tilted. The cross-sectional view in the accompanying diagram shows how the inner sides of the cylinders overlapped.

Another departure from conventional practice was the siting of the slide valves. They could not be placed above the cylinders, as in the I class, because there would have been insufficient room between the cylinders and the bottom of the smokebox; equally obviously there was no room between them, and the bogie made an underneath siting impossible. So they had to be sited outside the cylinders and outside the framing, where there was plenty of room. This imparted a very unusual appearance to the locomotive, the sides of the smokebox curving out above what looked like a square box on either side. From the point of view of the men in the repair and maintenance depot it was a very good idea, since once the cover plates had been removed the valves themselves were easy to get at. However, the gear which activated them, Joy's, as in the I class engines, was still inside the frames, working the valve spindles by means of rocker arms, and required the customary physical contortions when being serviced. This pattern of gear proved to be the Achilles' heel of this type of engine in its compound form, for components were continually cracking or breaking.

Other differences from the I class were the increase in heating surface and grate area, the larger firebox and the placing of the sandboxes over the fronts of the splashers. A large tender was fitted, holding almost 4,000 gallons of water. The first five of these engines had their steam

North Eastern Railway I and J class 4-2-2s

	I class		J class	
	As compound	**As simple after rebuilding**	**As Compound**	**As simple after rebuilding**
Dates of building or rebuilding:	12/1888–6/1890	1900–1902	8/1889–12/1890	1900–1902
Boiler – length:	10 ft 7 in	10 ft 7 in	11 ft 4 in	11 ft 4 in
width:	4 ft 3 in	4 ft 3 in	4 ft 5 in	4 ft 5 in
Total heating surface:	1,136.12 sq ft	1,136.12 sq ft	1,139 sq ft	1,139 sq ft
Grate area:	17.3 sq ft	17.3 sq ft	20.7 sq ft	20.7 sq ft
Boiler pressure:	175 lbs/sq in	175 lbs/sq in	175 lbs/sq in	175 lbs/sq in
Cylinders:	HP 18 × 24 in	18 × 24 in	HP 20 × 24 in	19 × 24 in
	LP 26 × 24 in		LP 28 × 24 in	
Wheels – bogie:	3 ft 7 in	3 ft 7 in	3 ft 7 in	3 ft 7 in
driving:	7 ft 1 in	7 ft 1 in	7 ft 7 in	7 ft 7 in
trailing:	4 ft 7 in	4 ft 7 in	4 ft 7 in	4 ft 7 in
Total wheelbase:	21 ft 11 in	21 ft 11 in	21 ft 11 in	21 ft 11 in
Weight of engine in working order:	43 tons	44 tons	46 tons 13 cwt	47 tons
Adhesion weight:	18 tons	18 tons	19 tons	19 tons
Tractive effort at 85% working pressure:		13,608 lbs		14,162 lbs

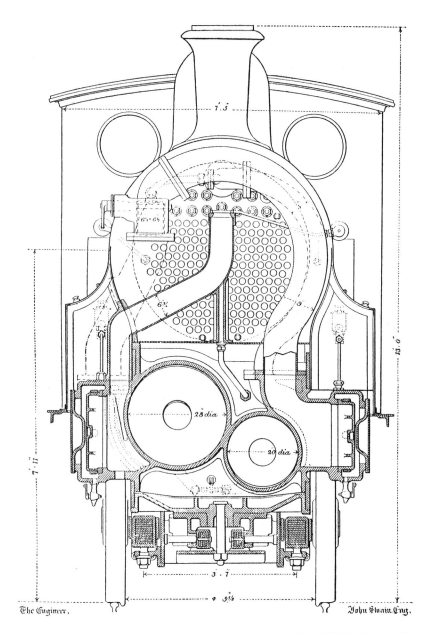

Cross-section through the front end of the NER 4-2-2 Class J two-cylinder compound, showing how the high- and low-pressure cylinders were placed relative to each other.
(*The Engineer*)

NER 4-2-2 two-cylinder compound No. 1518 of Class J, with 7 ft 7 in driving wheels. Note the rectangular cover beside and below the smokebox, behind which the cylinder valves were sited.   (*The Engineer*)

COMPOUND EXPRESS ENGINE, NORTH EASTERN RAILWAY.
MR. T. W. WORSDELL, GATESHEAD ENGINEER.

sandpipes directed only in front of the driving wheel tyres; the remainder were given pipes to the rear of them as well.

Both these classes of locomotive had short lives in their compound state. After T. W. Worsdell's retirement, his successor, Wilson Worsdell, allowed the building of the J class to continue, but after a few years converted

NER 4-2-2 two-cylinder compound, Class J, with 7 ft 7 in driving wheels, No. 1518.

By comparison, a two-cylinder simple rebuild, of No. 1520. Note the disappearance of the valve cover by the smokebox, and the provision of outside bearings to the trailing wheels. *(NRM)*

them to simple expansion working. Rebuildings began in January 1895 and were spread over twenty months. As compounds they had performed well enough on the road, but their valve gear had given trouble, as indicated above, and any savings gained from compounding had to be set against losses through the engines being laid up for repairs, and when these turned out to be excessive the reconstructions began. Nos 1254 and 1256 only lasted in their original form for $4\frac{1}{2}$ years and none remained unrebuilt for as long as seven years. Reconstruction involved the replacing of the existing cylinders by a pair of simple expansion cylinders, the replacing of the Joy valve gear and outside slide valves with Stephenson's gear and W. M. Smith's special piston valves with collapsible rings (as were now being fitted to the MR 'Spinners'), while outside bearings were given to the trailing wheels so that they were less likely to run hot from their proximity to the firebox. The appearances of the J class singles, before and after rebuilding, may be seen in the adjacent photographs.

The I class were left a little longer in their original state; reconstruction began in 1900 and was complete in 1902. The same changes were made as to the J class, except that the valves did not have to be re-sited. Only by peering beneath the boiler would the observer have noticed that there was any difference between the un-rebuilt and rebuilt engines, though the outside bearings to the trailing wheels would have given the game away.

In their rebuilt form the I class lasted until 1919/21, and the J class on average a year longer; none survived to be taken over by the LNER at the Grouping. The smaller engines did a little main line work between York and Edinburgh in their earliest days but were soon moved to work secondary expresses between Sheffield or Leeds and the Yorkshire coast resorts of Scarborough and Bridlington, as well as Hull. The J class did main line express work between York, Newcastle and Edinburgh for some years until increasing train loads forced their transference to join their smaller sisters, and by 1909 most of them were stationed at Scarborough.

✳ ✳ ✳

Of the day-to-day performances of the I class in their compound form nothing is known; a little is known of the J class, and that little is controversial. O. S. Nock, in his book *Locomotives of the North Eastern Railway*, writes approvingly of the Js and mentions two achievements of No. 1517 soon after it was built. On one occasion it took as much as 270 tons from Newcastle to Berwick-on-Tweed, 66.9 miles, in 78 minutes, and with a train of somewhat more than half that weight it attained 90 mph at an unspecified point on that section. The latter figure, though unlikely, is not impossible; Charles Rous-Marten once timed a MR 'Spinner' to reach 90 between Luton and Bedford on a 1 in 200 downhill gradient, and there is a similar racing stretch

between Newcastle and Berwick, the 16 miles between Christon Bank and Smeafield, towards the end of which it could have happened. The same stretch of line was used to carry out indicator trials with No. 1518 in 1889 in order to determine the best valve setting for the cylinders; at one point a speed of 86 mph was alleged to have been reached *on level track* with a train of 224 tons, when a horsepower indication of 1,069 was observed. Mr Nock, mentioning this, stops short of incredulity, merely saying that the figures were remarkable and that it would have been interesting to find out for how long such an effort could have been continued.

W. A. Tuplin, writing 15 years later, in his book *North Eastern Steam*, felt he could not accept the published figures and believed someone had made an error when using a slide rule. He was willing, however, to admit that this speed might have been reached at the foot of a long down gradient if there had also been a strong following wind. The report said that 86 mph had been reached on the level, but not that the previous acceleration had been on level track. If it did occur, Smeafield again seems the most likely location.

As to the regular running of these engines while in their compound state, the writer has been unable to discover any published records, but a certain amount is known about their performances after being rebuilt, and a little also about the I class. To deal with the latter first, Rous-Marten had something to say about them soon after all ten had been altered to simple expansion working; unfortunately (as, alas, so often) he is short on detail. Writing in *The Railway Magazine* in June 1902, he says:

"It has been the fashion to speak somewhat disparagingly of the earlier batch as altogether feeble and incapable machines. My own experience of them has not supported that unfavourable view. I have always found them do well even with very considerable loads ... One day, not long since, I had No. 1330 on the "Leeds-Scarborough Special", the fast express which leaves Leeds every evening at 5.05 and runs to Scarborough, $67\frac{3}{4}$ miles, in 75 minutes, passing through York without halting. The load was the usual light one of five bogie coaches, weighing in all 126 tons exclusive of engine and tender. No. 1330 made a very fine run, doing the journey from Leeds to Scarborough, start to stop, in 72 minutes 14 seconds inclusive, with a bad relaying slack at Waterloo Junction [soon after leaving Leeds] and a worse signal check at Huttons Ambo [three miles short of Malton], the latter very nearly a stop. The net time from Leeds to Scarborough was only $69\frac{1}{4}$ minutes, making no allowance for the regular service slacks at Church Fenton Junction, at York Station and round the Kirkham curves. This was one of the best runs I have had with that splendid train. A speed of 80.3 miles an hour was attained down the Micklefield bank, and the final stage of 42 miles from York (passing) to Scarborough (stop) was covered in 41 minutes 44 seconds net. The last 21 miles from Malton to the Scarborough stop occupied 20 minutes 40 seconds. All the prescribed service slacks were most strictly observed."

The doings of the rebuilt J class engines are better documented. During the 1895 'Race to Aberdeen' one of them alternated with a 4-4-0 on the racing train. E. L. Ahrons reported that on one occasion No. 1522, hauling 101 tons, reached Newcastle in six seconds less than the 80 minutes allowed in the racing schedule for the $80\frac{1}{2}$ miles from York to Newcastle by way of the High Level bridge across the Tyne. Thirsk (22.2 miles) was passed in 22 min 58 sec, Darlington (44.1 miles) in 42 min 54 sec; a bridge repair over Durham Viaduct was then experienced, but Durham was passed in 64 min 58 sec. No speeds are given. Rous-Marten also mentions a run on the first of the racing trains, when with a load of 180 tons No. 1518 made the journey in 86 minutes in spite of a 6-minute delay at Durham Viaduct, when the train was twice brought to a stand. Later, during 1904, he recorded a very fast run with a light load of 105 tons, when:

"... No. 1517 actually reached Darlington—passing dead slow owing to adverse signals—in 41 minutes 3 seconds from the dead start [at York]. A speed of 70 miles an hour was attained, on a slightly rising gradient[1], in eight minutes from the start, and 75 on a short downhill bit just before being slackened by signal approaching Darlington. Thirsk ... was passed in 21 min 54 sec, Northallerton, 30 miles, in 28 min 48 sec, and the final $14\frac{1}{4}$ miles to Darlington occupied only 12 min 15 sec. This was clearly brilliant ... The continuation of the journey to Newcastle was done, from the slow out of Darlington, in 39 min 45 sec for the $36\frac{1}{4}$ miles, the driver having to ease down as he had got much in front of his booked time."

Some time later, with 280 tons behind the tender, he noted a run in the opposite direction in which time was gained between Newcastle and York, though on an easier booking. The engine was No. 1522, which as noted above, had taken part in the 'Race to Aberdeen' of 1895. *"Starting away from Newcastle, No. 1522 sustained a minimum rate of 45 miles an hour up the rise of 1 in 150 past Plawsworth and 40 miles an hour up the 1 in 120 towards Durham, and Darlington was reached in 43 min 58 sec from the Newcastle start. Getting away again, we covered the $14\frac{1}{4}$ miles from Darlington in 15 min 49 sec, attaining at that point [ie at Northallerton] a speed of 67.4 miles an hour, which subsequently increased to a maximum of 70.5. The whole run of $44\frac{1}{4}$ miles from Darlington to York was done in 44 min 28 sec, representing practically the mile a minute average from start to stop. This with a load of 280 tons may be taken as showing that single wheelers can still do some very creditable work."*

Much later, in 1913, Cecil J. Allen, who had succeeded Rous-Marten as the principal reporter of locomotive performance in the columns of *The Railway Magazine*, was also writing approvingly of these engines, which were now only a few years short of their final withdrawal. In the December 1913 issue of the periodical he described runs made behind them on the secondary fast services to which they, together with the I class, had by then been relegated. On a Leeds to Bridlington evening business express, timed to cover the $63\frac{1}{4}$ miles in 73 minutes, signal delays were experienced outside Leeds and again before Selby, where the train was brought to a dead stand.

"Starting again after a stop of 25 seconds' duration, we had but 47 min 25 sec left for the last $43\frac{1}{4}$ miles ... Passing Selby, $\frac{3}{4}$ mile from the stop, in $2\frac{1}{4}$ min, we attained the mile a minute rate in three miles, and accelerated further to a maximum of 64.3 at Foggathorpe, so that the $17\frac{1}{4}$ miles from Selby to Market Weighton were covered in $18\frac{1}{4}$ min. The ascent of the Wolds was much finer [than in a previously mentioned run], Enthorpe, $3\frac{3}{4}$ miles from Market Weighton (passed slowly) being reached in $5\frac{1}{4}$ min, with a minimum speed as high as 41.1 miles an hour. The undulating grades beyond were traversed at speeds varying from 63.8 to 72.5 miles per hour, the $7\frac{1}{4}$ miles from Enthorpe to Southburn taking only 6 min 35 sec, so that ... timekeeping was practically assured with a clear road. But this was not to be, as after a cautious approach to Driffield we were stopped dead just east of the station on account of a goods train shunting just ahead. The $2\frac{3}{4}$ miles from Southburn to Driffield had taken $3\frac{1}{4}$ minutes; 35 seconds later we stopped for a brief $\frac{1}{4}$ minute, and the engine then gave us the finest exhibition of the journey, passing Nafferton, two miles, in exactly 4 minutes at 60 miles an hour, covering the $7\frac{1}{4}$ miles from Nafferton to Carnaby in 6 min 40 sec, and the distance of almost $11\frac{1}{2}$ miles from outside Driffield to Bridlington, start to stop, in $13\frac{3}{4}$ min ... The net time was not more than $70\frac{1}{2}$ min for the $63\frac{1}{4}$ miles.

Performances such as this, over a route now long disused between Selby and Driffield, were probably not made very often, and even more seldom recorded. The summit at Enthorpe was preceded, after the slack through Market Weighton, by $3\frac{1}{2}$ miles at 1 in 95/100, up which, to judge from the time taken from Market Weighton to the summit, the 41.3 mph minimum must have been maintained almost the whole way; this may be compared with the ascent of the last part of Beattock bank by CR No. 123 with a similar load (about 100 tons in both cases), when the rate fell to $36\frac{1}{2}$ mph.

However, Mr Allen reserved his superlatives for two runs on the Leeds–Scarborough line, on the same train in which Rous-Marten had timed the performance of an I class 7-foot single ten years earlier. The run to Bridlington just described, he said, was:

"... altogether overshadowed by two that I enjoyed on the Leeds–Scarborough "Limited" during the past summer. In both cases the load was only trifling, consisting of three 8-wheelers and totalling 85 tons, but the work of the 4-2-2 engine No. 1523, ably handled by Driver Goodwin of Leeds, is of such superlative merit as to call for tabulation. The first run, though fine, was not exceptional. A speed

1. Rous-Marten was in error as the line is dead level for nearly twelve miles between milepost 1 and milepost 13 out of York.

of 51.1 miles per hour was maintained up the 1 in 160 and 168 past Cross Gates, and then rose after a faint check at Micklefield to the very high figure of 80.3 miles per hour on the 1 in 132 descending to Church Fenton, where we eased considerably. A good speed was also maintained along the level stretch to York, the centre of which station was passed dead slow $\frac{3}{4}$ min ahead of time. Very fine work followed on the level stretch beyond, the engine accelerating rapidly to 67 miles per hour, which speed fell to 61.6 on the faint rise to Barton Hill. After the usual moderate rate on the curved 5-mile section, and a faint slack at Malton, brilliant running was made on the level stretch beyond Rillington, a speed of 73.8 miles per hour being maintained for miles, with a momentary maximum of 75 near Ganton. On this excellent run, therefore, $1\frac{1}{4}$ minutes were economised on schedule time.

These times, however, are completely eclipsed by those of the second run, which is one of the finest trips I have ever made behind a single wheeler, and demonstrated the speed capabilities of these remarkable engines to the very utmost. At the start the work was excellent, a speed of 52.9 miles per hour being attained on Cross Gates bank, while beyond Micklefield the terrific maximum of all but 85 miles per hour was sustained for an appreciable distance. I may say that this figure, and indeed all other figures of this journey, were checked by the stop watch of a Scarborough friend and co-enthusiast travelling with me, all of whose records on this train, as well as my own, went by the board on this memorable journey. At this tremendous speed the running was remarkably smooth, despite the very light load. Unfortunately we were checked severely by signals outside Church Fenton, but, accelerating with lightning rapidity, we were going at 73.8 miles per hour by the time we passed Copmanthorpe, despite the very faintly rising grade. A Midland express which had cheerfully steamed past us on the adjacent line at Church Fenton suffered the indignity of being overhauled and passed within the next two miles. By Chaloners Whin we had tied with the times of the first run, despite our check, and, running faster to York, were 20 seconds ahead at that point.

Gaining speed more rapidly, this had become 35 seconds ahead at Haxby, and thereafter the times of the first run were left altogether behind. On the level grades beyond Haxby we touched 71.4 miles per hour, and breasted the two miles at 1 in 295 and 309 past Flaxton at 68.1. From York to Malton in 23 minutes was a remarkably fine time, with so slow a start and the five miles of curves, but finer was to follow, as on the faintly undulating stretch to Ganton we actually touched 76.3 miles per hour, and so completed the 21 miles from Malton to Scarborough,

despite a signal check at Washbeck, in $20\frac{3}{4}$ minutes. With all checks we had gained 3 min 20 sec on schedule, but the net time could not have exceeded $69\frac{1}{2}$ minutes at the very most, and possibly 69 minutes, which means a gain of six minutes on this difficult booking. Driver Goodwin deserves the heartiest congratulations for this wonderful effort, which certainly constitutes one of my very finest runs of the year, and is entitled to take a front place in the ranks of even modern locomotive achievements."

North Eastern Railway J class 4-2-2 No. 1523, Leeds–Scarborough

Load: 85 tons gross

	Run No.	1			2		
		Actual time		Speed	Actual time		Speed
Miles		min	sec	(mph)	min	sec	(mph)
00.0	Leeds	00	00		00	00	
04.5	Cross Gates	07	30	51.1	06	50	52.9
09.8	Micklefield	12	55	68.1	12	10	73.8
				80.3			84.9
					sigs		
14.6	Church Fenton	17	10		17	00	
17.9	Bolton Percy	20	00	66.1	20	30	63.8
23.6	Chaloners Whin Junction	25	25	60.0	25	25	73.8
25.5	York	28	15		27	55	
29.6	Haxby	34	10	63.8	33	35	
34.5	Flaxton	38	50	67.0	38	00	71.4
36.8	Barton Hill	41	00	61.6	40	00	68.1
41.3	Castle Howard	45	45		44	40	
46.6	Malton	52	20		50	55	
50.8	Rillington	57	10	64.3	55	25	
54.8	Heslerton	60	40	73.8	58	50	73.8
59.6	Ganton	64	50	75.0	63	05	76.3
64.5	Seamer	69	00		67	15	
					sigs		
67.6	Scarborough	73	45		71	40	

The non-stop Leeds to Scarborough flyers were suspended during the First World War and briefly reintroduced when it was over, outlasting the single wheelers which had headed them for only a few years. There have not been any 75-minute non-stop bookings on this stretch of line since their time. Today, one 'Sprinter' diesel multiple unit train, running through from Liverpool, manages to do the journey in 80 minutes with a 3-minute stop at York and halts at Malton and Seamer, comfortably but without excitement. With the ability of the 'Sprinters' to accelerate from rest, no 80 mph speeds now need to be attained.

❋ ❋ ❋ ❋

8 The Great Western Bogie Single Wheelers—Masterpieces by Accident

During the last decade of the 19th century the Great Western Railway built 80 bogie single wheelers which, in the course of their rather short lives, achieved a splendid reputation and for some time were the company's chief express locomotives. Only the Midland built a larger number. They were extremely handsome in appearance and one of them made a speed record which stood for a long while. They looked like works of engineering art which were the product of a single concept in the mind of a mechanical genius. In fact, the first 30 were rebuilds, and eight of these were rebuilds of rebuilds; only the last 50 came straight from Swindon Works in their final form. Paradoxically, their perfection was the consequence of accident.

William Dean, the GWR Locomotive Superintendent who masterminded their design and production, had succeeded Joseph Armstrong in 1877 and continued his policy of using single wheelers on fast passenger services, rebuilding some of his engines but keeping to the 2-2-2 wheel arrangement. As the time for the abolition of the broad gauge drew near he began to build convertible locomotives with double frames, the wheels being outside both frames for use on the wider track but intended to be moved inwards on shortened axles for eventual use on the standard gauge. Dimensionally they were designed for the latter gauge, so that only the wheels and running boards needed alteration. In 1888 he built a number of 2-4-0s in this manner for use on the more hilly parts of the GWR system, to be altered later, and in 1891, when the broad gauge was on the verge of abolition, he constructed eight 2-2-2s for use on that gauge during its last few months; after that they too would be modified.

The accompanying line drawing shows the type as first built in side view. What strikes the eye is the way in which splashers have been obviated, the running board on either side curving over the leading, driving and trailing wheels so as to cover the tyres but not the spokes. This peculiar arrangement, which the above-mentioned 2-4-0s had also displayed, was of course

dictated by the imminence of alteration; there was no point in adding a lot of metal which would have to be removed again within a few months. All the axles were fitted with under-hung springs.

Another feature showing a variation from the previous custom was the raised upper outer cover of the firebox; the latter itself was not raised, but it was now possible to allow the water space above it, which was continuous with the tubular boiler in front, to have more room in which steam could collect just above the hottest part of the furnace. Dean, however, did not do the logical thing and collect the steam for the cylinders above the firebox, as Churchward was later to do, but employed a massive brass dome, which was the hallmark of his designs, which he placed on the second ring of the boiler and a little ahead of the line of the driving axle. No other single wheelers had more attractive domes than the GWR ones; they were always kept brightly polished and were their most prominent feature. (It was not uncommon for an otherwise perfect photograph of one of these engines to be spoiled by the dome refusing to show up on the negative, since it reflected as much light as the sky behind.)

The boiler was larger than those of previous standard gauge 2-2-2s, being made longer rather than wider since it had to fit between the 7 ft 8 in driving wheels after the adaptation had been made. This brought the smokebox further forward and increased the weight on the leading wheels. Another change from the usual practice was the placing of the valves beneath the cylinders, with their spindles inclined upwards towards the driving axle. This was because the diameters of the cylinders, each of 20 inches, did not permit the positioning of slide valves between them. Stephenson's valve gear was used, as with all other GWR engines before and since. The brake rods came across the outer sides of the driving wheels, which

A line drawing of the GWR Dean 2-2-2 single wheeler, No. 3021, as built for the broad gauge in 1891 and intended for later conversion to standard gauge.

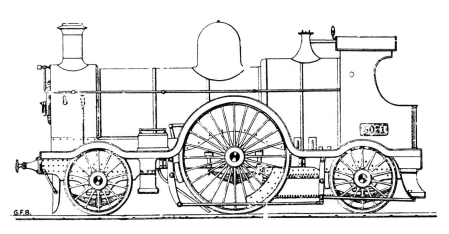

GWR 2-2-2 Dean single No. 3006 *Courier* before rebuilding as a 4-2-2.   (*Photomatic*)

detracted a little from their appearance, but, in the case of the engines in their broad gauge form, did not matter very much, for they were not otherwise very graceful. In his book *Historical Steam Locomotives*, O. S. Nock refers to them as "a truly horrible hotch-potch." However, they did not long endure in their original form.

Nos 3021–3028 were built during 1891 but, with the gauge conversion less than half a year away, the next two emerged from Swindon looking very different—not yet beauty queens but a good deal more sightly than before—and built for the standard gauge. A further 20 followed, and the first eight were rebuilt to match them once the last broad gauge rails had been removed from

the line from Paddington to Penzance, the former old-style broad gauge engines being then lined up for scrapping at Swindon.

One could now see what Dean envisaged as being the main line express locomotive of the immediate future. The new-style single wheeler had no bogie, despite the fact that other main lines were using bogie singles with success. Dean had not been fortunate in his previous essays in designing a leading bogie, and two of his attempts to do so had met with disaster. With any leading bogie there was the double question of whether, on the one hand, it could carry the front of the engine

GWR 2-2-2 Dean 2-2-2 No. 3009 *Flying Dutchman* as built in March 1892, before conversion to a 4-2-2 in 1894.

(*Photomatic*)

stably and firmly, while on the other hand it would not be so rigidly pivoted to the frame as to damage the rails on a curve, or even become derailed itself. What mattered was where it should be attached to the frame and what degree of controlled side play should be given.

When Dean first tried to design a bogie, his intention seems to have been to avoid a central pivot pin at all costs. The one he placed on an experimental 4-4-0 tank engine in the middle 1880s was so eccentric in its design as to have no firm attachment to the engine frame at all. The weight of the locomotive was taken upon springs, from which the bogie hung (or would have hung if the whole engine had been raised in the air) so that there was scarcely any side control at all. It proved a complete failure. However, ten years later he would learn wisdom and his first 4-2-2s and 4-4-0s would be given leading bogies which caused no trouble at all.

The new 2-2-2s and the eight which had been modified had double framing and bearings with the wheels between the outer and inner frames; whereas they had previously been almost flush with the cab sides, they were now 14 inches further in towards the centre line. They retained their outside springs, which were still under-hung, looking to a later eye accustomed to third-rail electric traction almost like collecting shoes, so close did they reach to rail level. Large semicircular splashers covered the upper parts of the driving wheels, where the locomotive's name appeared on curved brass plates. The running boards arched over the driving axle bearings like those of the Midland 'Spinners'. A shallow splasher covered the tops of each of the front carrying wheels. Otherwise there was not much change. Whereas the eight oldest in their broad gauge condition had been given tenders displaced from former broad gauge engines, which were not at all handsome objects, having prominent outside plate springs reaching half-way up their tank sides, all 30 in their standard gauge form had tenders with springs immediately above the outside wheel bearings, and the tank sides were smooth and continuous, with the GWR monogram in the centre and coal rails added at the top.

The new locomotives seemed to be satisfactory replacements for the withdrawn broad gauge express engines. The larger boilers made them quite heavy engines, the adhesion weight of each being as much as 19 tons. To allow flexibility on curves, the leading wheels were allowed two inches of side play, and this, together with the greater weight placed upon them than was usual, may have contributed to the unfortunate accident which occurred on 16th September 1893, which was potentially very serious though fortunately there was no loss of life. No. 3021 *Wigmore Castle*, the first of the re-gauged convertibles, was derailed while hauling an express train at speed inside Box Tunnel. The line here is straight (it is said that on one day of the year—traditionally Brunel's birthday—the rising sun shines right through the tunnel from its eastern end), so the mishap had nothing to do with curvature. It appears that the large boiler, projecting forward upon the frames,

GWR 4-2-2 Dean single No. 3021 *Wigmore Castle* after two reconstructions, first from broad gauge 2-2-2 to standard gauge in 1892, and again from 2-2-2 to 4-2-2 in March 1894. This was the engine which had an accident while traversing Box Tunnel, as a consequence of which it and its 29 sister engines were all converted to 4-2-2s.

GWR 4-2-2 Dean single No. 3005 *Britannia*, after rebuilding from a 2-2-2. Seen at Westbourne Park in April 1902.
(Ken Nunn Collection, LCGB)

made the locomotive over-heavy at the front end and caused unsteadiness at speed.

It was decided to equip the whole class with a front bogie. The damaged engine was the first to be thus rebuilt, and the others followed suit. Meanwhile, the first of a further 50 was under construction, and this, and its fellows, emerged complete with front bogies, one by one, from Swindon between March 1894 and March 1899.

The bogies with which they were fitted proved thoroughly successful and gave no trouble. Similar ones were later given to the 4-4-0s which began to come out at the end of the decade, including the famous 'Cities' which proved to have a turn of speed superior to that of any single wheeler when they were put to it. Dean came round to the idea of having a central swivelling pin, controlled on either side by coil springs, and used a long wheelbase so that the bogie was stable on the track and did not tend to move crab-wise. It was also constructed

GWR No. 3014 *Iron Duke*, at Old Oak, after reconstruction from a 2-2-2 in 1894.   *(Photomatic)*

GWR Dean 4-2-2 No. 3036 *Crusader*, built in September 1894.
(*Photomatic*)

in such a way that the removal of a few bolts enabled it to be rolled clear from underneath the engine when the front of the latter was sufficiently raised; this made it easy to get at the valves which were immediately under the cylinders. Large outside plate springs above the axleboxes also made for smooth running.

Over the five years during which the Dean 4-2-2s were being built at Swindon, while there was a general likeness between them all, there were some differences in detail. The first 30 engines, originally built as 2-2-2s and which had been reconstructed as 4-2-2s by the forward exten-

sion of their frames and running plates, had under-hung trailing wheel springs; with the later 50, the springs of these wheels were placed above the axles and outside the cab sides. The clack boxes and the pipes carrying the feed water through them to the boiler changed their positions more than once as new engines emerged. At first the former were very prominent, sited almost half-way up either side of the boiler and about a foot from the rear edge of the smokebox, with the pipe leading to it slanting upwards from below, but from the end of 1897 it was

GWR No. 3050 *Royal Sovereign*, built in February 1895, seen at Westbourne Park. Note the front bogie, fitted experimentally with helical springs. (*Photomatic*)

brought outwards and vertically upwards on either side. Later still the clack boxes were placed inconspicuously on the underside of the boiler and could not be seen at all.

From the end of 1897, also, the remaining new engines were built with slightly extended smokeboxes, which were later fitted to the whole class. So far as internal details were concerned, the most important change made when the later 50 were built was the provision of smaller cylinders, the diameter changing from 20 inches to 19 inches; the previous 30 later had their own cylinders lined up to match. From 1898 the whole class, one by

one, was given slightly thicker wheel tyres, which enlarged their diameters by half an inch. Other slight alterations are noted in the complete list of locomotives at the end of this chapter.

Quite a number of these locomotives were modified during the 1900s, being fitted with domeless boilers of the kind developed by Churchward after he had succeeded Dean as Locomotive Superintendent at Swindon. Their appearances were certainly not improved by the change. As to their performance, not much evidence remains; they were now in their declining years, being insufficiently powerful to be employed on the most

GWR 4-2-2 No. 3067 *Duchess of Teck*, as built in December 1897.

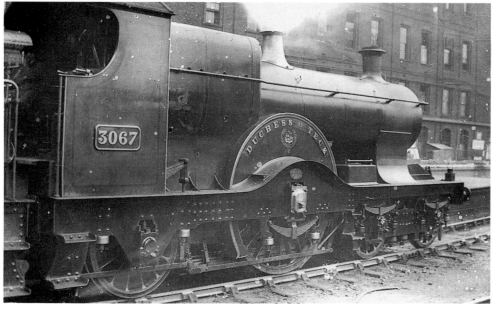

No. 3067 *Duchess of Teck* but as rebuilt by Churchward with a domeless parallel boiler and Belpaire firebox in March 1906.

(*Photomatic*)

GWR 2-2-2 'Queen' class No. 1123 *Salisbury*, also rebuilt by Churchward with a domeless parallel boiler and Belpaire firebox. (*P. W. Pilcher Collection, NRM*)

important expresses, which were now much heavier than before. Churchward had been building 4-4-0s and 4-6-0s which turned out to be much better able to cope with the increased loads. Probably Dean built many more singles than were really needed. Details of the various re-boilerings are given in the accompanying list.

In their heyday the liveries of the Dean singles were perhaps more splendid than any other British main line could offer. Boilers, fireboxes, cab sides and tenders were painted in Brunswick green; splashers, running boards and outside frames were in Indian red. The domes, safety valve covers and splasher beadings were of brass, polished until it shone. The nameplates along the top edges of the splashers were also of brass, but were painted black except for the letters themselves, so that the names showed up brilliantly. On the centre of each splasher was a metal plate depicting the GWR coat of arms. The locomotive's number appeared on a rectangular cast plate on each cab side. Each tender bore the GWR monogram in copperplate script letters in the centre of each side. For the most part the engines carried sonorous names, many transferred from former broad gauge express locomotives; later on, quite a few were re-named to avoid confusion with named engines of other classes.

The period of greatest fame of the Dean singles was the dozen or so years ending in 1904, when one of them set up a record by running from Bristol to Paddington in less than 100 minutes. During the last few years of the 19th century they had the main line from Paddington through Bristol to Newton Abbot virtually to themselves and headed all the principal expresses. Fortunately we are well supplied with details of their performances, some of which will now be described.

* * *

One may begin with an account by Charles Rous-Marten of a journey behind No. 3029 *White Horse* on an express to the West of England, a non-stop run from Paddington to Exeter on the 194-mile route by way of Bristol (the shorter route by way of Westbury not having yet become available), and booked in 223 minutes. The driver had expressed doubt about whether he would be able to keep time (though the load, about 120 tons, was not heavy) since because of extensive track relaying a great many checks were to be expected.

"No time was lost in getting over the earlier stages of the journey. Some remarkably quick travelling was made in the beginning, Slough (18½ miles) being passed in 19 min 29 sec, and Taplow East Box (22 miles) in 22 min 48 sec.

Here, however, the first check was encountered, a train in front having been allowed to remain in the way, so that adverse signals caused our speed to be reduced to 5 miles an hour and a stop seemed inevitable. This was just escaped, and we proceeded on our way, but at Sonning (33¾ miles) met a second similar check. A third was experienced at Reading and a fourth before Tilehurst, the speed in each case going down to 5 or 10 miles an hour. Ill fortune still stuck to us, for at Didcot a fifth signal slack reduced the speed to 15 miles an hour, and we had hardly recovered from this when a sixth check brought us down to 20 miles an hour at Steventon. With such disastrous luck a good run seemed hopeless. Still, we had done that 56½ miles from London in 66 min 5 sec in spite of the six slacks. And now the driver did some splendid work up the ascending grades of 1 in 660, covering the distance, just under 17 miles, all uphill, from Wantage to Swindon in 16 min 58 sec.

Swindon was passed at full speed in 88 min 20 sec from London. This, in view of the six bad checks encountered, is a more remarkable performance than it would appear at first sight, for the loss of time was at least 13 minutes, and probably more, so that the run evidently could have been made with ease in 75 or 76 minutes or less, and it may be observed that a speed of over 60 miles an hour was maintained on the heaviest part of the distance, that after Didcot.

In the ordinary course some of the lost time would have been made up in the subsequent descent of the Wootton Bassett bank, but unfortunately extensive repairs were being carried out on a bridge about half way down the

Dean single No. 3040 *Empress of India*, built in September 1894, leaving Paddington on a semi-fast train in 1908.

(*Ken Nunn Collection, LCGB*)

incline, and the effect was to bring about another prolonged slackening to 5 miles an hour through Bath station, which was passed in 2 hrs 0 min 57 sec from the start. Water had been picked up once near Goring, and was taken again just before the train diverged from the main line to the curved deviation loop round Bristol. Temple Meads station was breasted in just 2 hrs 15 min from Paddington. After the main line was rejoined the driver, undismayed by all the adverse conditions with which so far he had had to contend, once more put his iron steed hard at it, and some excellent progress was accomplished, the next 35 miles after Bedminster being run in 34 min. But here, at Fordgate Crossing box, another check was experienced, and it was followed by yet one more at Durston, while Taunton station was rounded by the deviation line at barely 10 miles an hour.

By this time all hope of a punctual arrival seemed to have departed, but the driver and his 'White Horse' still pushed on resolutely. The Wellington bank was smartly ascended, the speed never going below 41 miles an hour up the rise of 1 in 81, and then came a brisk descent, without any exceptional maximum speed, towards Exeter, but with yet another passing check by signal near Stoke Canon. It was with some surprise, after all the hindrances experienced, that I found the train in Exeter station just 5 min 2 sec before time, the whole run of 194 miles having been accomplished in 3 hrs 36 min 25 sec, notwithstanding ten bad checks for signals or relaying, besides the three slowings through Bath and round Bristol and Taunton. The loss by signals, etc., amounted to fully 21 minutes . . . Thus, if the train could have made a clear run free of incidental delays but with the three service slacks, the journey would have been done in 3 hrs 15 min . . . Warren, the driver, deserved great credit for the smartness with which he worked the train through in spite of all these

serious obstacles, finally landing it at Exeter five minutes before time, and this without resorting to any exceptional speed down the banks."

This run was made when the Dean single wheelers were still the GWR's principal express passenger engines. But the building of the 4-4-0 'Armstrongs' had already begun, to be followed by the 'Badmintons', 'Atbaras' and 'Cities'. During the early years of the 20th century many of the 4-2-2s were transferred to work the Birmingham expresses from Paddington. Though not really competitive with the London & North Western service between these cities, the trains were quite smartly timed and no doubt carried many business people for whom Paddington was more convenient of access than Euston. Overall times varied between Paddington and Birmingham; 140 minutes or a little more was general.

During 1901 Rous-Marten experienced an excellent performance by No. 3051 *Stormy Petrel* on the 9.30 am from Paddington, which with a load of about 230 tons would have almost kept time to Birmingham had there not been a signal check at Bordesley a mile short of Snow Hill station; the schedule was 143 minutes. He published a log of the journey, which included no speeds, but one can infer from it that speeds were in the 60s, rising to about 65 mph between Southall and Reading, and fell away into the upper 50s between Reading and Didcot, not rising above 58 beyond Oxford and reaching no more than 65–66 on the descent to Leamington, where the engine was being worked easily, perhaps to fill the boiler. Up the 1 in 107 of Hatton bank the minimum was 33 mph, and between there and Solihull 60 may just have been reached. With a faster descent of Southam bank and the absence of the Bordesley stop time might just have been kept. One gets the impression that the

engine was being worked to just about the limit of its capacity. Reading was passed in 39 min 17 sec, Didcot in 56 min 42 sec, Oxford in 68 min 17 sec, Banbury in 93 min 8 sec and Leamington in 113 min 33 sec; Bordesley, where the train was stopped by signals, was reached in 142 min 20 sec.

On the same train and at about the same time, Cecil J. Allen enjoyed a much faster run behind one of these locomotives (he does not say which one) with a load of 175 tons, when time was gained despite a faster schedule and a signal stop at Bordesley such as Rous-Marten had experienced. The times are given to the nearest quarter-minute and no speeds are indicated, but one can deduce that the latter were in the middle and lower 60s all the way from Slough to Didcot, and that a much faster descent was made of Southam bank. From Paddington to Slough took 22 minutes; Reading was passed in $39\frac{1}{4}$ minutes, Didcot in 56 minutes, Oxford in 66 minutes, Banbury in 89 minutes, and Leamington in $107\frac{1}{2}$ minutes, where a coach slipped, reducing the load to 150 tons. The $6\frac{1}{4}$ miles from there to Hatton took only $7\frac{1}{2}$ minutes and, despite the halt at Bordesley, Snow Hill was reached in 136 minutes from Paddington, or 134 minutes net.

Details of a much finer run than either of the above were published by Rous-Marten in *The Railway Magazine* for April 1908, timed by a correspondent. The engine was No. 3010 *Fire King*, the load was 175 tons to Leamington, where two coaches were slipped, and the weather was bad, with a strong wind and, after Oxford, drizzling rain which made the rails slippery. Only two speeds are given, the maximum near Southam Road being $76\frac{1}{4}$ mph and the minimum up Hatton bank was $47\frac{1}{2}$ (the load now being reduced to about 125 tons). From the log other speeds can be approximately de-

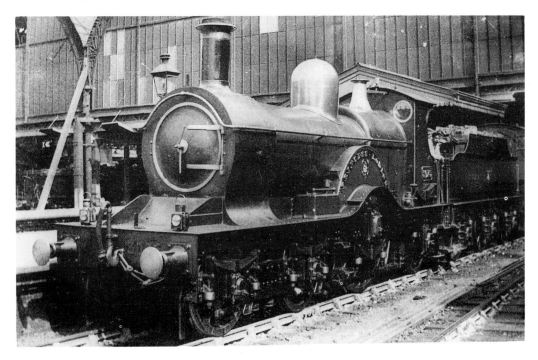

Dean single No. 3075 *Princess Louise*, built in July 1898, about to leave Paddington on a semi-fast train. *(Photomatic)*

duced; Southall was passed at about 60 mph; nearly 70 was reached at Slough; from there to Reading speed varied in the middle 60s; and onwards to Didcot it fell away to about 60, the side wind probably being most strongly felt here.

Beyond Oxford there was a bout of slipping which brought the speed well down, but it had recovered to about 65 before Aynho. On the last lap past Solihull 70 may have again been approached, and Snow Hill was reached in $1\frac{1}{2}$ minutes before time. Rous-Marten characterized it as, "an excellent run . . . highly characteristic of the type and class of the locomotive that performed it . . . The single driver Great Westerns have usually in my experience done good, steady average work pulling considerable loads at fair rates of speed without attaining very remarkable velocities." Somewhat faint praise, one feels. The log of the run was as follows:

Miles		Min	Sec
00.0	Paddington	00	00
05.7	Ealing	08	00
09.1	Southall	11	23
13.2	West Drayton	15	28
18.5	Slough	20	18
24.2	Maidenhead	25	44
31.0	Twyford	31	56
36.0	Reading	36	30
41.5	Pangbourne	41	44
44.7	Goring	44	54
48.5	Cholsey	48	43
52.8	Didcot E Junc	53	22
58.3	Radley	59	03
63.4	Oxford	64	34
69.0	Kidlington	71	23
73.3	Heyford	79	34
80.3	Aynho	85	15
86.2	Banbury	91	36
89.8	Cropredy	95	53
95.0	Fenny Compton	103	03
106.0	Leamington	113	54
	(2 coaches slipped)		
112.2	Hatton	121	00
118.9	Knowle	128	26
122.3	Solihull	131	59
124.8	Acock's Green	134	23
129.3	Birmingham	138	31

The slow average speed between Kidlington and Heyford was due to a bad bout of slipping on wet rails.

Without any question the greatest recorded achievement of any Dean Single wheeler was the feat performed by No. 3065 *Duke of Connaught* when it headed the "Ocean Mails Special" on 9th May 1904 from Pylle Hill Junction, Bristol, to Paddington, 118.4 miles, in $99\frac{3}{4}$ minutes, the train consisting of four vans weighing 120 tons. The load, while light, was no lighter than these engines were expected to haul on many of the scheduled services, and the astonishing speeds maintained by the engine for mile after mile between the slack at Cricklade Bridge and the outskirts of Paddington show that Rous-Marten was

hardly being fair when he said that "remarkable velocities" were not to be expected from these engines. His own complete log of the journey is given below. Its most astonishing feature is the maintenance of an average of 80 mph from Shrivenham to Westbourne Park, 70.2 miles, over a road which was either level or only very slightly downhill, with an engine lacking the front-end refinements on valve design such as the 'Castles', which later worked the "Cheltenham Flyer", were to possess. Nothing similar was achieved over this stretch of line until the days of the latter train after its final acceleration, when a train only twice as heavy was hauled by a locomotive of three times the power of Dean's single wheeler. An indication of how *Duke of Connaught* was being extended is seen in the average speed between Box and Corsham, just over 60 mph, *after* the slack through Bath and *up* $2\frac{1}{2}$ miles at 1 in 120/100. After the slowing beyond Swindon, speed remained between the upper 70s and the lower 80s the whole way, with peaks of about 85 mph near Challow and $83\frac{1}{2}$ near Slough.

Miles		Min	Sec
00.0	Pylle Hill Junc	00	00
01.4	Bristol E. Junc	03	39
04.6	Keynsham	07	21
07.0	Saltford	09	32
11.5	Bath*	13	38
13.8	Bathampton	16	00
16.5	Box	18	28
20.1	Corsham	22	01
24.4	Chippenham	25	48
30.7	Dauntsey	30	49
35.5	Wootton Bassett	35	06
41.1	Swindon	39	37
41.5	Cricklade Bridge*	40	31
46.9	Shrivenham	45	19
51.9	Uffington	49	17
54.5	Challow	51	09
58.0	Wantage Road	52	47
61.9	Steventon	55	40
65.3	Didcot	58	08
69.9	Cholsey	62	40
73.6	Goring	65	21
76.8	Pangbourne	67	52
79.3	Tilehurst	70	06
82.0	Reading	72	09
87.0	Twyford	76	00
93.8	Maidenhead	80	58
95.6	Taplow	82	11
99.5	Slough	85	03
101.7	Langley	86	40
104.4	West Drayton	88	56
106.7	Hayes	90	39
108.5	Southall	92	07
110.2	Hanwell	93	22
111.0	West Ealing	93	59
111.9	Ealing	94	38
113.4	Acton	95	40
116.3	Westbourne Park	97	01
117.6	Paddington	99	46

*Passed very slowly

As already noted, a number of these engines were given new boilers by Churchward, losing their magnificent brass domes and acquiring Belpaire fireboxes. The first to suffer this change was No. 3027 *Worcester*, which underwent its metamorphosis in March 1900. In 1903 Rous-Marten recorded a fine performance behind it, which he described in the columns of *The Engineer*:

"The engine on this occasion took the Cornish express from Exeter to Bristol, and undoubtedly made an excellent run, ascending the 20 uphill miles from Exeter to the Whiteball Summit in 26 min 3 sec, although her load was nine of the large bogies, or over 230 tons behind the tender. The grade along the last $2\frac{1}{2}$ miles before the summit is at 1 in 115 continuously. Up this stretch the single wheeler with her new boiler managed to maintain a minimum speed of 39.1 mph.

Taunton, $30\frac{3}{4}$ miles, was passed in 35 min 23 sec from Exeter—exceptionally quick time for that distance. The final $44\frac{3}{4}$ miles from Taunton to Bristol occupied 47 min 4 sec, the driver being obliged to ease down, else he would easily have covered that distance on a nearly dead level road at the even mile a minute. As it was, we ran from Exeter to the Bristol stop, $75\frac{1}{2}$ miles, in 82 min 27 sec."

It is a pity that the maximum speed on the descent from Whiteball was not given, as it must have been high. *City of Truro* the following year, when reaching 100 mph or more near Wellington, took only a minute less over this stretch, though it began the descent at a much higher speed than *Worcester* and had a much lighter load. It is

pleasant to record that No. 3027 was returned to something much more like its original appearance on its second re-boilering, being given its dome back, though still retaining a Belpaire firebox.

Finally, some examples may be given of the running of the Dean 4-2-2s in their later years. An anonymous contributor to *The Railway Magazine* in 1911 wrote an article about the class as a whole, in which he included four logs of journeys on the 9.10 am from Bristol to Paddington on various occasions between 1906 and 1910. Between Bath and Paddington the train was scheduled in 115 minutes—not a very demanding timing, but the interest lies in the efforts made to recover lost time. His table of logs, somewhat modified, is given here.

On the first journey, No. 3001 *Amazon* with a 125-ton load gained time steadily until just before Reading, but then suffered a long and severe permanent way slowing. After making a good recovery, the engine was again on time at Ealing, then signal checks made it six minutes late into Paddington. Between Chippenham and Swindon, which included the $1\frac{1}{2}$ mile ascent of Dauntsey bank, the average speed was almost 61 mph, and from Swindon to Didcot over 68 mph. When stopped at Westbourne Park the train was four minutes ahead of schedule.

On the second journey, No. 3072 *Bulkeley*, with a similar load, was a little slower to Swindon, but suffered checks on approaching Didcot and when passing through. Fast running then put the train ahead of time at Ealing, but another signal check at Old Oak made the

Dean singles, Bath–Paddington, 1906–10

		1/11/06		6/9/07		20/9/09		23/4/10	
Date:									
Locomotive No.:		3001		3072		3049		3043	
Load (tons):		125		125		150		125	
Miles		**Min**	**Sec**	**Min**	**Sec**	**Min**	**Sec**	**Min**	**Sec**
00.0	Bath	00	00	00	00	00	00	00	00
05.0	Box					08	15	08	00
						sigs			
12.9	Chippenham	17	45	18	00	17	45	17	05
								sig	stop
24.0	Wootton Bassett					28	00	32	00
								pws	
29.6	Swindon	34	15	35	00	33	45	38	15
								pws	
43.0	Challow					46	45	53	45
				sigs (×3)		sigs			
53.8	Didcot	55	30	59	00	56	30	64	00
						sigs			
62.2	Goring					69	30	71	35
			pws						
70.9	Reading	73	15	78	15	77	30	79	25
88.4	Slough	90	30	94	15	93	00	94	55
								pws	
97.8	Southall							107	30
						sigs			
101.2	Ealing			106	15	107	30	111	15
		sig	stop	sigs				sigs	
		& delays							
106.9	Paddington	121	00	115	45	116	15	120	45

Dean single No. 3066 *Duchess of Albany*, built in December 1897, here seen double heading a train about to leave Bristol, Temple Meads; the other locomotive is No. 3815 *County of Hants*. *(NRM)*

arrival at Paddington $\frac{3}{4}$ minute late. The average speed between Reading and Ealing was about 68 mph along virtually level track.

No. 3049 *Nelson*, rebuilt with a domeless boiler and Belpaire firebox, and hauling a six-coach load of 150 tons, passed Swindon $2\frac{3}{4}$ minutes early despite a slight check just beyond Box, but was badly delayed on both sides of Didcot. Time recovery then began and an early arrival was within sight, but a series of checks at West Drayton, West Ealing, Royal Oak and Westbourne Park brought the train into Paddington $1\frac{1}{4}$ minutes late. The Chippenham to Swindon stretch was covered at an average of $62\frac{1}{2}$ mph, and that from Goring to Slough at about 67 mph. This was probably the best run of the four, though it has to be observed that it was the only one in which fine weather and dry rails were experienced.

On the last run, No. 3043 *Hercules*, hauling 125 tons, put up a dogged fight against adversity. It was halted for over a minute at Wootton Bassett, slowed to 30 mph through Swindon and again to 15 mph through Shrivenham, but made up time rapidly from there to just short of Southall, covering the 52 miles from Challow to milepost 12 at an average of about 65 mph. It then met a disheartening sequence of checks which made the

arrival at Paddington nearly six minutes late. It is difficult to calculate net times for these runs, but in all cases they must have been well below the scheduled time, and the whole sequence reflects credit on a class which, though long outmoded, still worked some of the best expresses at the end of the Edwardian decade.

The first of the Dean single wheelers to be withdrawn from service were Nos 3005 *Britannia* and 3020 *Sultan*, in February 1908; both had been originally built as 2-2-2s. The last to go were Nos 3050 *Royal Sovereign* and 3074 *Princess Helena*, in December 1915, both after having been re-boilered and given Belpaire fireboxes. It is a great pity that none was preserved—*Duke of Connaught* surely merited survival—but their scrap value outweighed any sentimental appeal. Actually, Churchward had proposed to rebuild some 30 of them as 4-4-0s with 7 ft 2 in driving wheels, but the reconstruction when costed appeared to be uneconomic. During the course of their active lives many had been re-named, in some cases to avoid confusion with more recently built 'Saint' and 'Star' 4-6-0s; others merely had their nameplates removed. The longest lived was No. 3027 *Worcester*, originally named *Thames*, which had started its life as a broad gauge 2-2-2, been twice rebuilt and then twice re-boilered, and not withdrawn until July 1914 after a life of almost 23 years. The shortest lived was No. 3079 *Thunderbolt*, the last but one to have been built in February 1899 and withdrawn in September 1911.

We can however still admire their graceful lines as an

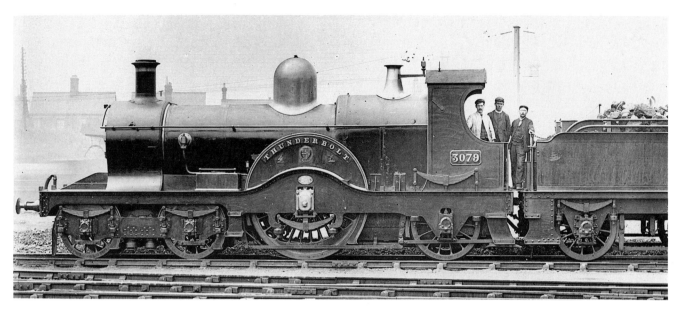

excellent, but non-working, full-size replica has been constructed. This portrays No. 3041 *The Queen* and forms part of the Royalty & Empire exhibition at Windsor & Eton Central Station.

The shortest lived of the GWR singles, No. 3079 *Thunderbolt*, built in February 1899, withdrawn September 1911.
(*P. W. Pilcher Collection, NRM*)

GWR 4-2-2s Nos 3001–3030 and 3031–3080 (as built or as reconstructed for standard gauge)

	Nos 3001–3030	Nos 3031–3080
Dates of construction (or reconstruction):	Nov 91–Aug 92	Mar 94–Mar 99
Wheel arrangement:	2-2-2	4-2-2
Boiler – length:	11 ft 6 in	11 ft 6 in
width:	4 ft 2 in	4 ft 2 in
Length of firebox:	6 ft 4 in	6 ft 4 in
Heating surface – boiler:	1,342 sq ft	1,434 sq ft
firebox:	123 sq ft	127 sq ft
total:	1,465 sq ft	1,561 sq ft
Grate area:	20.8 sq ft	20.8 sq ft
Boiler pressure:	160 lbs per sq in	160 lbs per sq in
Cylinders:	20 in × 24 in	19 in × 24 in
Wheels – leading:	4 ft 7 in	
leading bogie:		4 ft 1 in*
driving:	7 ft 8½ in	7 ft 8½ in*
trailing:	4 ft 7 in	4 ft 7 in
Total wheelbase:	18 ft 6 in	23 ft 6 in
Weight in working order:	44 tons 4 cwt	49 tons**
Adhesion weight:	19 tons	18 tons
Tractive effort at 85% of working pressure:	14,115 lbs	12,738 lbs

*From 1898 thicker tyres were fitted to the whole class, including those rebuilt from 2-2-2s, and each diameter was increased by ½ inch.
**When Nos 3001–3030 were reconstructed as 4-2-2s their weight rose to 48, not 49 tons.

GWR 4-2-2 Locomotives

Number	Name	Boiler alteration/renaming
3001	*Amazon* *	
3002	*Atalanta* *	
3003	*Avalanche* *	
3004	*Black Prince* *	Type DO, Apr. 1906
3005	*Britannia* *	
3006	*Courier* *	Type BR 5, Sept. 1910
3007	*Dragon* *	
3008	*Emperor* *	
3009	*Flying Dutchman* *	Type BR 5, Sept. 1911
3010	*Fire King* *	
3011	*Greyhound* *	
3012	*Great Western* *	
3013	*Great Britain* *	Type DO, Nov. 1906
		Type BR 5, Oct. 1910
3014	*Iron Duke* *	
3015	*Kennet* *	Type BR 0, Sept. 1902
3016	*Lightning* *	Type DO, Dec. 1906
3017	*Nelson* *	Re-named *Prometheus*, May 1895
3018	*Racer* *	Type DO, Nov. 1906
		Type BR 5, Dec. 1911
		Re-named *Glenside*, Sept. 1911
3019	*Rover* *	
3020	*Sultan* *	
3021	*Wigmore Castle* **	
3022	*Rougemont* **	Re-named *Bessemer*, 1898
3023	*Swallow* **	
3024	*Storm King* **	
3025	*St George* **	Re-named *Quicksilver*, May 1907
3026	*Tornado* **	

Above: GWR 2-2-2 Dean single No. 3018 *Racer*, as built in April 1892. Also converted to a 4-2-2 in August 1894.

Below: GWR 4-2-2 No. 3019 *Rover*, after reconstruction from 2-2-2 configuration.   (*Photomatic*)

Number	Name	Boiler alteration/renaming	Number	Name	Boiler alteration/renaming
3027	*Thames***	Type DO, Mar. 1900 Type BR 5, Mar. 1911 Re-named *Worcester*, Dec. 1895	3033	*Albatross*	Type DO, Nov. 1906
			3034	*Behemoth*	
			3035	*Bellerophon*	Re-named *Beaufort*, Dec. 1895
3028	*Wellington***		3036	*Crusader*	
3029	*White Horse**		3037	*Corsair*	
3030	*Westward Ho**		3038	*Devonia*	
3031	*Achilles*		3039	*Dreadnought*	Type DO, Apr. 1906 Type BR 5, Mar. 1911
3032	*Agamemnon*	Type BR 5, Mar. 1911			

Number	Name	Boiler alteration/renaming	Number	Name	Boiler alteration/renaming
3040	Empress of India				Type BR 5, Aug. 1911
3041	Emlyn	Boiler pressure raised to 180 lb/sq in, Dec. 1912			Re-named Lambert, July 1901
		Re-named The Queen, 1897	3056	Timour	Type BR 5, July 1910
		Re-named James Mason, June 1910			Re-named Wilkinson, July 1901
3042	Frederick Saunders	Boiler pressure raised to 180 lb/sq in, June 1909	3057	Tartar	Re-named Walter Robinson, July 1901
3043	Hercules	Boiler pressure raised to 180 lb/sq in, June 1909	3058	Ulysses	Type DO, Nov. 1906
		Type BR 5, Apr. 1911			Re-named Grierson, May 1895
3044	Hurricane		3059	Voltigeur	Re-named John W. Wilson, Mar. 1908
3045	Hirondelle	Boiler pressure raised to 180 lb/sq in, June 1909	3060	Warlock	Type BR 5, June 1911
		Type BR 5, Sept. 1911			Re-named John G. Griffiths, Mar. 1909
3046	Lord of the Isles		3061	Alexandra	Re-named George A. Wills, Oct. 1911
3047	Lorna Doone				
3048	Majestic	Type DO, Apr. 1906	3062	Albert Edward	Boiler pressure raised to 180 lb/sq in, June 1909
		Type BR 5, July 1910			Type BR 5, Aug. 1911
3049	Prometheus	Type BR 0, Oct. 1901	3063	Duke of York	
		Type BR 5, Aug. 1910	3064	Duke of Edinburgh	
		Re-named Nelson, May 1895	3065	Duke of Connaught	Type BR 5, Dec. 1910
3050	Royal Sovereign	Type BR 0, Feb. 1909	3066	Duchess of Albany	Type BR 5, June 1911
		Type BR 5, Feb. 1914	3067	Duchess of Teck	Type DO, Mar. 1906
3051	Stormy Petrel				Type BR 5, Sept. 1910
3052	Sir Walter Raleigh	Type DO, Mar. 1906	3068	Duke of Cambridge	
		Type BR 5, Mar. 1911	3069	Earl of Chester	
3053	Sir Francis Drake		3070	Earl of Warwick	Type DO, Sept. 1905
3054	Sir Richard Grenville				Type BR 5, June 1910
3055	Trafalgar	Boiler pressure raised to 180 lb/sq in, July 1909	3071	Emlyn	Type BR 5, Nov. 1910

GWR 4-2-2 No. 3063 *Duke of York*, built in June 1897.

(NRM)

Number	Name	Boiler alteration/renaming
3072	*North Star*	Re-named *Bulkeley*, Sept. 1906
3073	*Princess Royal*	
3074	*Princess Helena*	Type BR 5, Nov. 1911
3075	*Princess Louise*	
3076	*Princess Beatrice*	
3077	*Princess May*	
3078	*Shooting Star*	Re-named *Eupatoria*, Aug. 1906
3079	*Thunderbolt*	Type DO, Mar. 1906
3080	*Windsor Castle*	Type BR 5, July 1910

Note re boiler provision

The type of boiler originally fitted was classified as R 51; the dome was slightly to the front of the line of the driving axle and the firebox had a raised round top.

Boiler type BR 0 was domeless, not coned, and with a raised Belpaire firebox.

Boiler type DO was domeless, not coned, with a raised Belpaire firebox, and attached not to the usual curved-side smokebox but to a drumhead one.

Boiler type BR 5 was domed, with a raised Belpaire firebox and a drumhead smokebox.

*First built as 2-2-2s (standard gauge) before alteration to 4-2-2s.
**First built as 2-2-2s (broad gauge) before alteration first to standard gauge 2-2-2s, then to 4-2-2s.

Dean 4-2-2 No. 3056 *Wilkinson*, built in March 1895 and then named *Timour*, but renamed in July 1901, leaving Paddington with a semi-fast train.

(*Photomatic*)

9 The 'Double-Singles' of the London & South Western

What constitutes a single wheeler is perhaps a matter of argument, and it would be possible to contend that the engines dealt with in the present chapter should not be so described since they each had four driving wheels. However, they lacked coupling rods, and in effect each one was two single wheelers on one frame with one source of steam. One was built for the LSWR at Nine Elms Works in 1897 and five more in 1901. Nothing else like them ever appeared again on any British railway. They have had few champions and many detractors. Cecil J. Allen, in one of his *Railway Magazine* articles, admits that on one occasion, when travelling westwards from Waterloo, he avoided boarding a train hauled by one and took the next train instead—and duly found that his train was being delayed by the tardy running of the one in front. How good or bad these locomotives really were will be considered later; first one needs to discuss why they were built at all.

Dugald Drummond, Locomotive Superintendent of the LSWR from 1895 to his death in 1912, was a hard-headed Scot as well as being a brilliant railway engineer. He had given the Caledonian Railway the best and most economical passenger express engines it had ever had when he left that company's service in 1890 to try his luck in Australia, and the LSWR Board was glad to be able to command his services in place of William Adams when the latter retired in 1895. In return he built them many excellent 4-4-0s, some 4-6-0s which were not so outstanding, and a large number of tank engines, some of which were still running in 1964, 67 years after the first of their type had been built. But brilliant engineers sometimes make mistakes, as F. W. Webb did with his three-cylinder compounds on the London & North Western, and the latter went on compounding his errors (if the pun will be forgiven) whereas Drummond did not—and his six 'double-singles' were never as bad as Webb's worst failures.

Drummond does not seem to have been either sentimentally or practically inclined towards the single wheeler as a type. After the two he built for the North British Railway in 1876 (which were almost replicas of Stroudley's first 2-2-2, *Grosvenor*—see Chapter 2) he built no more, though he was probably consulted regarding the building of CR No. 123 (Chapter 6). So far as passenger locomotives were concerned, he was a 4-4-0 man, until towards the end of his career when he tried his hand with dubious success at designing four-cylinder 4-6-0s to cope with the LSWR's increasing passenger loadings. He certainly did not share Patrick Stirling's belief that large single driving wheels were a good idea, since none of his engines had driving wheels in excess of 6 ft 7 in except for the two early 2-2-2s. The 'double singles' of 1897 and 1901 appear quite out of character. Why then did he build them?

It is possible that when he returned from Australia in 1895 and became au fait with the contemporary scene in Great Britain he was impressed with what the newly built single wheelers on the MR and GWR were actually doing. D. L. Bradley, in his book *The Drummond Greyhounds of the LSWR*, considered that:

"Drummond was greatly impressed by their speed, free running and economic working, although at the same time considering that the loads and gradients of the Bournemouth line called for more adhesion than was possible with a single set of driving wheels. This apprehension was overcome in a 'double single' design, in which two inside cylinders drove the leading driving wheels and the outside pair the trailing drivers. With the absence of coupling rods the wheel arrangement became 4-2-2-0."

This is quite possible, and one also has to consider the attitude of the LSWR's Board of Directors, whose members will have been well aware that their company's rival for the West of England traffic was running its best expresses with 4-2-2s in the early 1890s. The LSWR's main line to the West, however, was too steeply graded beyond Salisbury to compare with that of the GWR as far as Newton Abbot. East of Salisbury (except on the direct Portsmouth line through Haslemere) gradients were easier—certainly no worse than those on the MR south of Derby. There might have been scope for a few 4-2-2s on this part of the system. Certainly the Board had been leaning rather heavily on Drummond's predecessor, who in 1893 had submitted to them completed drawings of an 8-footer with outside cylinders. But nothing further was done during his superintendency, and it was left to Drummond to take up the challenge.

He submitted his design for a 'double-single', which was not at all in the traditional style. Apart from the doubling of the number of driving wheels and the provision of both inside and outside cylinders, it was different in being, for its time, a really big engine, larger and heavier than most 4-4-0s he or anyone else had so far built, yet having driving wheels of only 6 ft 7 in diameter. The Board was persuaded that he was fulfilling its wishes and gave him the go-ahead. One argument he may very well have used to obtain this consent was that such a locomotive would not require a pilot engine when the load became heavy—in contrast to Webb's three-cylinder compounds which were always having to be piloted. In effect each 'double-single' would be two single wheelers working in tandem, but only needing one pair of men on one footplate, thus saving money in wages.

The first 4-2-2-0 to emerge from Nine Elms in August 1897, No. 720, at once caught the eye of all interested in locomotive development, for it was unique in a number of respects—and, so far as the LSWR was concerned, unique also in having four cylinders instead of the usual two. The first thing to impress the beholder would have been the long boiler, which included a firebox 8 feet in length in a boiler extending for 20 feet from smokebox to cab. The next thing to strike the eye would have been

Dugald Drummond's first 'double-single', No. 720, as originally built and painted in Stroudley's dark ochre livery. The absence of water troughs on the LSWR system was the reason for the large eight-wheeled tender. *(NRM)*

the tender, running on eight inside-sprung wheels, with high sides and coal rails that reached almost to the level of the cab roof; it looked almost too large for the engine. The provision of such a huge tender was of course due to the absence of water troughs on the LSWR main lines. With one of these 'water carts', as they were irreverently termed, a non-stop run of over 100 miles—eg from Waterloo to Bournemouth—was a possibility; otherwise stops of five minutes or more would have been necessary to fill the tender tank.

Probably the next thing to be noticed would have been the small outside cylinders well back along the frames and driving on the rear wheels, and the outside Joy valve gear operated from the connecting rod, the cylinders having their valves beneath them, the whole assemblage reminding one strongly of the outside motion of Webb's three-cylinder compounds. Above the driving axles the careful observer would have noticed something quite anomalous—separate coupling rod splashers outside the driving wheel splashers, though there were no coupling rods for them to cover. Next it would be seen that the bogie wheels also had a neat continuous splasher on either side, like Stirling's 8-footers. Finally, if the by-stander remained long enough to hear it, there was an

LSWR 4-2-2-0s Nos 720 (1897) and 369–373 (1901)

	No. 720		Nos 369–373
	As first built	As finally rebuilt	
Boiler – length:	12 ft	12 ft	12 ft
diameter:	4 ft $5\frac{1}{8}$ in	4 ft $10\frac{3}{4}$ in	4 ft $5\frac{1}{8}$ in
Firebox – length:	8 ft	8 ft	8 ft
Heating surface (sq ft) – firetubes:	1,307	1,392	1,344
firebox water tubes:	215	195	190
firebox surface:	142	173	156
Total:	1,664	1,760	1,690
Grate area (sq ft):	27.5	27.5	27.5
Boiler pressure (lbs/sq in):	175	175	175
Cylinders:	15 in × 26 in	14 in × 26 in	14 in × 26 in
Wheels – bogie:	3 ft 7 in	3 ft 7 in	3 ft 7 in
driving:	6 ft 7 in	6 ft 7 in	6 ft 7 in
Total wheelbase:			
Weight in working order:	54 tons 11 cwt	60 tons 1 cwt	58 tons 14 cwt
Adhesion weight – front drivers:			
rear drivers:			
Tractive effort at 85% of working pressure:	22,030 lbs	19,190 lbs	19,190 lbs

organ pipe whistle which emitted a deeper and more sonorous note than the usual high-pitched ear-splitting variety.

So much for visible alterations in structure. As to appearance, the livery had also been changed from the familiar LSWR green. No. 720 emerged from the works clothed in Stroudley's dark ochre and with 'LSW' on its tender instead of 'LSWR'. The former may have been a tribute to his old chief's memory; the reason for the latter no one ever knew. The rest of the engine was pure Drummond, smokebox wing plates and all.

There were also unusual features which did not strike the eye. In the first place, the inside valve gear was different from that on the outside, being the customary Stephenson type. These actuated the valves of the cylinders driving the leading crank axle. Completely undetectable to the eye, however, unless one put one's head through the firehole door, were the cross water tubes placed transversely across the upper part of the firebox. This feature, which Drummond was subsequently to use in all his express locomotives, was an attempt to achieve a larger heating surface in the hottest part of the furnace.

In all steam locomotives the greater part of the total heating surface consisted of the inner sides of the many tubes that carried the products of combustion from the firebox to the smokebox. It can readily be appreciated that the temperature at any part of these tubes would be the less in proportion to the distance from the firebox throatplate, the gases being cooled by the boiler water around them and having less heat to give up the further they travel. So the most effective boiling of water occurs at the top, sides and front of the firebox. However, if tubes are placed across the interior of the firebox near the top, and *their* interiors are made continuous with the inside of the boiler, so that they too are filled with water,

a very considerable addition of boiling space is provided where the fire is hottest. It is obvious how great a help to efficient steaming such a device could be; the only question is whether added difficulties of maintenance might outweigh the advantage. This was later found to be the case, and Drummond's successor, Robert Urie, removed the cross water tubes from all the former's engines as they came in for rebuilding.

The tubes were inclined from one side to the other so that the bubbles of steam, as they formed, could travel sideways and upwards towards the water spaces at each side of the firebox. This seemed to Drummond a neat and effective way of maximizing the heating area—much more effective than clogging up the main boiler with fire tubes. The water tubes could be cleaned out from their ends when the locomotive was serviced. In No. 720, as originally constructed, it was necessary to remove the boiler cladding to do this; in later engines Drummond fitted rectangular covers on either side of the firebox so that the tubes were more accessible.

On 26th August 1898, *The Engineer* published a photograph of the new engine a year after its completion, when it had been run in and undergone some trials, and added a few observations, terming the engine "the most original in design that has been produced since Mr Webb's first four-cylinder compound." The firebox was "enormous" and had "no less than 357 square feet of the finest heating surface imaginable, of which 215 are due to the transverse inclined water tubes." The reversing gears could be operated "almost with the finger and thumb . . . We have only to add that the engine is quite realising all that Mr Drummond anticipated, and appears to provide a most satisfactory solution of the heavy fast train problem."

In this sanguine judgement *The Engineer* was certainly

One of the later 'double-singles', No. 371, built in 1899, leaving Waterloo with a semi-fast train. Note the box covering access to the cross water tubes on the firebox side.
(*Photomatic*)

mistaken. Almost from the start difficulties began to be met. The enginemen from all sheds where it travelled made complaints. They did not like it at all and feared it would be the forerunner of many more. Drivers of steam locomotives, whatever their political views might have been, were conservative in their working habits, and Drummond was still a new broom sweeping clean after the easygoing régime of his predecessor. In particular he was trying to train his enginemen into managing their charges by adjusting the cut-off instead of using the regulator, making better use of the steam's expansive power in the cylinders and so saving coal. Later he came to be more appreciated, but at this stage he was still eyed with suspicion.

In September 1897, a month after the locomotive had first appeared, he called a special meeting of senior drivers and tried to explain and justify the new ideas exemplified in No. 720. The men listened politely but were not convinced, and later asked for another meeting. What pleased them most at the latter was the news that the next ten engines to be built at Nine Elms would be 4-4-0s of a more conventional pattern. None the less, Drummond did not promise to withdraw the offending engine; instead he had its cylinders lined up to a $14\frac{1}{2}$ instead of 15 inches diameter in an attempt to make it steam better, and later was to give it a larger boiler. Discontent with it remained, however, and the surprising thing is that he built another five. One wonders why—if the engine was a good one, why not build many more; if bad, why any more at all? Perhaps it was a manifestation of a 'Scots wha hae' spirit, the William Wallace in

him coming out in a clash with the Southrons. At least he could claim to have saved his face and gained a little ground; if this was not Bannockburn, at least it was not Flodden Field.

* * *

Some records exist of the running of No. 720 in its original form. On 19th May 1898 it was put at the head of the 9.30 am semi-fast from Waterloo to Bournemouth and a careful record was made mile by mile of its progress. The load was 300 tons, heavy for the time. Stops were made at Surbiton, Woking, Basingstoke, Winchester, Eastleigh, Southampton West, Lyndhurst Road, Brockenhurst, Hinton Admiral and Bournemouth East (now Pokesdown). A speed of 46 mph was reached before the Surbiton stop, 50 beyond Weybridge, 55 near Hook. From Basingstoke speed slowly rose up the gradient to Litchfield Tunnel and down the long 1 in 249/257 until 77 was attained before shutting off steam for Winchester; 67 was again reached before Eastleigh. No further mile-a-minute maxima were recorded on the six further start-to-stop stages until Bournemouth was reached. It was not an heroic performance, but time was kept, and possibly the object was to see how much water and fuel were used.

Two quite interesting accounts exist of its perform-

LSWR diagram of the performance of Drummond prototype 'double-single' No. 720 with a 300-ton load on the 9.30 am semi-fast, Waterloo to Bournemouth, 19th May 1898.

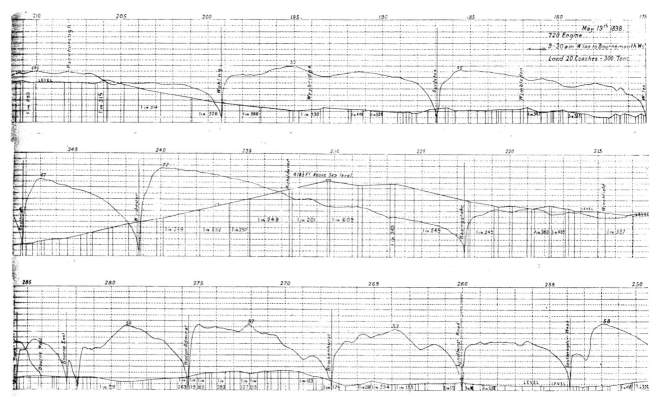

DIAGRAM OF SPEEDS AND INCLINES, WATERLOO TO BOURNEMOUTH

ance in ordinary service before it was rebuilt with a larger boiler; both are complimentary in tone, although in the second there is an undertone of suggestion that its usual behaviour was nothing to write home about. The first comes from *The Engineer* in the course of a leading article whose purpose was to protest that trains were becoming too heavy. A special boat train was instanced, taking travellers from Waterloo to Southampton Docks to embark for America, and troops to be shipped to South Africa to fight in the Boer War which had recently broken out. The load was estimated as at least 400 tons behind the tender.

"Viewed from the footplate, the train leaving the terminus 'looked like the side of a street'. The boiler pressure was 175 lbs and for the greater part of the run, made to Southampton without a station stop, the safety valves were on the point of blowing, or blowing lightly. The performance of the engine left nothing to be desired, and the consumption of coal was very moderate, as proved by the lengthened intervals between firing. The rate of running was extremely steady, post after post being passed at about forty-five miles an hour. For thirty miles out of the seventy-nine the run is all uphill, the line rising for seven continuous miles, on the Basingstoke and Woking section, at the rate of 1 in 249. Again, there are eleven miles, from the 20th mile on the Brookwood section, which rise continuously at the rate of 1 in 326, 314 and 304. Up the long bank through Basingstoke to the summit at the Litchfield tunnel the speed fell off a little; no matter for wonder when the enormous weight of the train and the wind and the rain are considered. But once over the hill the engine was left to have her own way, and sixty miles an hour was reached and maintained with great ease. The putting on of the mail vans caused the train to start three minutes late, and four minutes were lost at Queens Road by permanent way signals, but it reached Southampton at 1.40 pm, thus making up time on the road."

While there is nothing to enthuse about in this performance—a Drummond "Greyhound" would no doubt have done as well—it is interesting as a sign of what No. 720 could do when extended.

The second account comes from Rous-Marten's article in *The Railway Magazine* in April 1903.

"It may reasonably be expected that I should say something about the four-cylinder non-compound engines introduced by [Drummond] ... I have as yet seen so little of their work that I do not feel justified in pronouncing any definite opinion upon their capacity in actual practice ... It must suffice, therefore, to quote the best run I had with the first-built, No. 720. This took the 3 pm express from Waterloo to Salisbury. The load consisted of 7 eight-wheelers and 2 six-wheelers. It was given to me officially as 183 tons empty or slightly over 200 tons loaded ... Our hopes of being favoured with a clear through run without a check were speedily damped, for adverse signals brought us to a dead stand for all but 2 minutes at Queens Road. Getting away again we made good progress and got through Woking in 34 minutes 54 seconds inclusive from

the Waterloo start, or in 30 minutes' net time allowing for the signal delay. Up the 11 miles' continuous ascent at about 1 in 300 from a point near Weybridge almost to Sturt Lane junction our speed never fell below 52.6 miles an hour. The distance of $23\frac{1}{2}$ miles from passing Woking to passing Basingstoke, nearly all being on rising grades, was covered in 26 minutes 21 seconds, representing an average of 54.2 miles an hour. After passing Basingstoke good progress continued to be made in spite of rising gradients, and the next length of 19 miles was covered in exactly 21 minutes.

Immediately beyond Andover we encountered a bad relaying slack which cost us more than 2 minutes. We then soon recovered our speed, and down the falling gradients by which Salisbury is approached, just before steam was shut off for the final slow-in, we had attained our maximum rate, 76.3 miles an hour. Our inclusive time from Waterloo to Salisbury, start to stop, was 1 hour 42 minutes 43 seconds, but as we were at a dead stand for 1 minute 57 seconds, and as the delays, due to extra starting and stopping, and to a bad slow for relaying, amounted to $5\frac{1}{4}$ minutes, carefully computed, it will be seen that our net time from Waterloo to Salisbury was $95\frac{1}{2}$ minutes—a clearly creditable performance."

Whether or not the run was creditable as a whole, the last few miles certainly were. We are not told to what extent the train was slowed beyond Andover for the permanent way check, but if it came at the foot of the incline to Grateley, which steepens to 1 in 165 for almost 3 miles, the time of $20\frac{1}{2}$ minutes for the final 17.4 miles from Andover to Salisbury, which included the check and the recovery from it, was extremely good, and it is a great pity that the speed achieved on the rise to Grateley Summit was not given.

However, from an operational point of view, No. 720 remained unsatisfactory despite all attempts to put it right. Between January 1900 and August 1902 it was taken out of service eight times for periods totalling over ten months, for repairs and alterations. A wider cab and wide wheel splashers were fitted (the unnecessary coupling rod splashers now disappearing), alterations were twice made to the blast pipe, new tyres of Bessemer steel were fitted to the wheels, new inside cylinders 14 inches in diameter were supplied in place of the $14\frac{1}{2}$-inch ones and the outside ones were lined up to the same width, while double slide bars for the piston rods replaced the original single ones. The organ pipe whistle was removed and one of the ordinary type fitted in its place. The original livery was soon replaced by the usual green, the Board having disapproved of the dark ochre finish. Finally, between November 1903 and March 1905, it was laid up to receive a new boiler 5 feet in diameter.

In the meantime, five more 4-2-2-0s had been constructed in 1901, generally similar to No. 720 but with the wider splashers and with rectangular inspection covers on the firebox sides to allow easier access to the cross water tubes. The cylinders were 14 inches in diameter, the total heating surface was slightly increased

No. 369, one of Drummond's subsequent batch of 'double-singles', which differed from the prototype in having a larger boiler, wider wheel splashers and inspection covers on either side of the firebox which gave access to the cross water tubes.
(*NRM*)

and more weight was placed on the driving wheels. The total weight of each engine was 3 tons more than that of the prototype. A peculiarity was that the sand blast was directed down between the bogie wheels, an alteration difficult to understand in a locomotive type which had proved so prone to slipping; in 1905 this appliance was removed and replaced by gravity sanding directed under the driving wheels. The outside valve gear was made stouter and double slide bars were provided.

Between 1901 and 1904 all six were used on the expresses from Waterloo to Salisbury and Bournemouth, taking turns with the "Greyhounds" and the older outside-cylindered Adams 4-4-0s. Later, however, they were mainly confined to special duties, such as running troop trains and ocean liner specials and other secondary work, and were laid up during the winter months, so earning the soubriquet of "Butterflies". All were found to be very heavy on coal and oil.

They never steamed well—not even No. 720 after being given its 5 ft boiler—and continued to slip badly. The enginemen never liked them, although with experi-

ence they learned how to get the best out of them. At what point Drummond came to the conclusion that, whatever they should have been in theory, they were failures in practice, one does not know. Presumably he washed his hands of them when they were relegated to minor duties. It is interesting, however, to see some of their features being included in his first 4-6-0s, such as the cylinder positioning and the long firebox—and these engines, too, did not fulfil expectations, turning out to be enormous but rather lazy elephants when given express trains to handle.

Some records, though not many, remain of their work in the *Locomotive Performance* articles of *The Railway Magazine*, and only those of the prototype reflect credit on the engine. Evidently by the end of the decade they were being pressed into service again on fast expresses; on one occasion Cecil J. Allen timed the rebuilt No. 720 on a run from Basingstoke to Vauxhall, when it almost managed to make a start-to-stop run at a 60 mph average despite the handicap of a strong side wind. The 33 miles between Hook and Malden were covered in $30\frac{3}{4}$ minutes with a maximum of $72\frac{1}{2}$ mph between Woking and Byfleet. This was actually a better performance than any recorded of the newer 4-6-0s in the same article. In December 1916 he described a still better run between Waterloo and Salisbury, made during the previous summer, when, in Allen's words, "exceedingly fine work

Drummond 'double-single' No. 371 on a semi-fast Waterloo–Southampton train via Alton. (*Photomatic*)

LSWR No. 373 at Nine Elms after the removal of the cross water tubes from the firebox. (*Photomatic*)

was done". The load was 260 tons. After a fast start the 19.9 miles between Hampton Court Junction and Farnborough were covered in 20 min 10 sec, all uphill, with a minimum of 50 mph at milepost 31. By Basingstoke the engine was $2\frac{3}{4}$ minutes ahead of time on the 91-minute schedule, and maintained this lead to Salisbury with a maximum of 75 mph at Andover. One notes that on this and on the previous run the same driver's name is given; evidently with someone at the regulator who understood his engine, satisfactory performances from the point of view of timekeeping could be obtained—though this is not to say that they were satisfactory from the point of view of fuel consumption.

All six engines were withdrawn during 1926/7. They were an interesting experiment, and the two last quoted performances suggest that the rebuilt No. 720 was not as bad as it was made out to be. It does not seem to have occurred to Drummond to fit them with coupling rods, which would have kept the cylinders in phase with each other. Possibly he felt that the use of such long rods would not be safe. Superheating, too, might have improved them. As it was, most of them ended their days working light trains from Waterloo to Southampton by way of Alton and the 'Watercress Line'. It is a pity one could not have been preserved and be set to work there now—but no one preserves failures.

10 The Great Eastern Oil-Burners

For many years the Great Eastern Railway had bought single wheelers, first 2-2-2s and then 4-2-2s, from private manufacturers or had built them at Stratford Works for express passenger work. However, they had been supplemented by coupled engines which were perhaps more suitable machines for a company with a switchback main line whose gradients, though short, were in places quite steep.

The railway had originally been laid out with an eye to cheapness of construction, and this was especially seen in the avoidance of the use of tunnels where possible. Whereas, for example, the neighbouring Great Northern had twelve tunnels on its main line from King's Cross to Doncaster, including seven on the ascent to Potters Bar, on the GER main lines they were conspicuous by their absence. Of none of the other main lines out of London could this be said, and the price was paid in a saw-tooth gradient profile, with a 1 in 70 exit from Liverpool Street and innumerable short steep inclines in both directions, particularly on either side of Ingrave Summit, approached from London by three miles averaging about 1 in 100. It was not, on the face of it, a suitable line for single wheelers.

James Holden, however, who succeeded T. W. Worsdell as Locomotive Superintendent at Stratford Works in 1885, bowed to the prevailing fashion once steam sanding gear became available, and after introducing a 2-4-0 type with 7 ft coupled wheels and a disfiguring stove-pipe chimney, and setting out to construct them in large numbers, he carried out experiments with one of them, much as Johnson had done on the Midland, removing the coupling rods to see how it would function as a single wheeler. This locomotive was dispatched to Cambridge, to work over the more or less level road through Ely, March, Spalding, Sleaford and Lincoln to Doncaster, where Massey Bromley's 4-2-2 single wheelers had been spending their last years. It coped successfully with the trains it was given, so he then built another ten, this time as proper 2-2-2s with small rear wheels but otherwise similar to the 2-4-0s, and sent some to Norwich and the rest to Harwich for main line haulage.

Rous-Marten, in a report on 'British Express Engines' prepared for the International Railway Congress held in 1898, spoke highly of their performance, remarking especially that when it came to uphill work they could pull better than the 2-4-0s, though they did not seem to run as fast downhill—the opposite of what might have been expected. E. L. Ahrons, in his sequence of articles on *Locomotive and Train Working in the Latter Part of the Nineteenth Century*, published in *The Railway Magazine*, cites a friend's account of an experimental journey made behind one of these single wheelers on a 'down' express to Cromer:

"The load was approximately 170 tons. There was a strong side wind, and immediately after starting an adverse gradient of 1 in 70 [Bethnal Green bank] had to be faced, but the engine took the load up this bank with the utmost ease ... Later, ascending the gradient of 1 in 84 near

Brentwood, a speed of 31.1 mph was maintained. In spite of four bad checks for signals and relaying, which caused a delay of fully 7 minutes, Ipswich (68¾ miles from London) was passed in 83 min 49 sec, and the distance of 114 miles from London to Trowse Junction occupied 134¾ min, from which 9 min should be deducted for delays by 5 slackenings ... The performance was exceedingly good for an engine with relatively small traction force taking a considerable load over a heavy road with a strong side wind blowing. On the return journey with the same engine and train the speed rose to 70 mph several times, as against a maximum of 65.4 on the down journey, and the train had reached a point 15 miles from London 7 mins before time, but subsequent signal slacks absorbed all this gain. The distance of 99 miles from passing Trowse swing bridge at a slow walking pace to the signal check at Harold Wood was run in 112 mins ... On another occasion one of these engines kept time from London to Colchester with an express of 20 six-wheeled coaches weighing about 260 tons, the inclines of 1 in 70 and 1 in 84 being ascended without difficulty."

With such performances being achieved on the fastest trains of the GER it is perhaps not so very surprising that Holden should decide to follow the trend of the time and build ten bogie single wheelers which could be expected to do even better than these 2-2-2s. These were Nos 10–19, which emerged from Stratford Works in 1898. Their advent saw the beginning of the withdrawal of the 2-4-0s; these were gradually taken off main line duties, and the bogie single wheelers, along with the 'Claud Hamilton' 4-4-0s, whose construction began in 1900, replaced them, the former being quite soon displaced by the latter and sent in their turn to do duty on the easier Fenland routes beyond Cambridge.

These new locomotives were extremely handsome in appearance. There was a definite resemblance between them and the MR 'Spinners' and the GWR 4-2-2s. They had the same pattern of double frames, with the running plates arching over the outside bearings of the driving axles; the cabs were similar to the MR cabs, as was also the external plate springing on the driving and trailing wheels. As with most of the MR engines the dome was a little forward of the line of the driving axle; it differed from both the other types in not being crowned with a safety valve and not being of polished brass. The driving wheels, too, were only 7 feet in diameter. As if to make amends for the stove-pipes fitted to his earlier engines, Holden gave Nos 10–19 most handsome chimneys with copper caps.

However, the most noticeable and unusual feature of these engines, during most of the time that they were running, was their tenders. These were constructed, as were those of a number of other GER locomotives, to hold not only coal and water, but oil fuel as well, since they were designed to run on the latter once the fire in the firebox had been started and got going. These were the only 4-2-2s to be fuelled in this manner, and the

Great Eastern Railway oil-burning 4-2-2 No. 17. Built in 1898 this engraving shows the sturdy construction, roomy cab and asymmetrical placing of tender wheels.   (*The Engineer*)

practice calls for some explanation and comment.

The oil was not obtained from any refinery but was the waste product of gas-making plants. Hard to believe as it may now seem, the East London gasworks were in the habit, once they had processed their coal into saleable coke and gas, of discarding the still-remaining oily residues as waste, simply pumping it into the river! Holden conceived that instead of merely being expelled to pollute the environment (not that *that* would have worried the late Victorians greatly) it could be burned in the fireboxes of his locomotives in place of coal. He organized the regular purchase of the waste product and stored it in tanks near Stratford, at the same time adapting some of his locomotives to burn it, and for many years this fuel was widely used on the GER until the producers began to demand such high prices that using it became uneconomical.

The system by which it was burned in locomotives required that the fire in the firebox should be started in the usual manner. Once the grate had been covered by a layer of glowing coal the oil supply would be turned on to feed the firebox furnace. The oil was brought by pipes from the tender tanks, which terminated in burners sited beneath the footplate; these blew the oil, under the

GER oil-burning 4-2-2 No. 10, also built in 1898.   (*NRM*)

GER 4-2-2s Nos 10–19, built in 1898

Boiler – length:	11 ft
diameter:	4 ft 3 in
Firebox – length:	7 ft
Heating surface – firetubes:	1,178.5 sq ft
firebox surface:	114.23 sq ft
total:	1,292.73 sq ft
Grate area:	21.3 sq ft
Boiler pressure:	160 lbs per sq in
Cylinders:	18 in × 26 in
Wheels – bogie:	3 ft 9 in
driving:	7 ft
trailing:	4 ft
Total wheelbase:	22 ft 9 in
Weight in working order:	48 tons 10 cwt
Adhesion weight:	19 tons
Tractive effort at 85% of working pressure:	13,639 lbs

pressure of steam from the boiler, over the grate, where it ignited. In each burner were two separate steam pipes, one to inject the oil as a spray, the other to atomize its particles before they finally left the nozzle. In its final form (for Holden made many experiments), a burner, of which each locomotive had two, resembled that shown in the adjacent diagram. A contemporary description in a *Railway Magazine* article read as follows:

"All the injection cones (in each burner) are arranged in

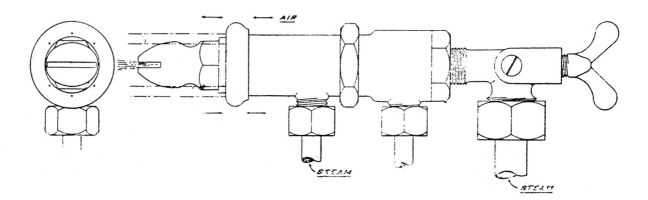

Diagram of J. Holden's patent burner for oil fuel locomotives.

a case, to which the oil fuel and steam connections are permanently made; and, should the interior become blocked, damaged or in any way rendered useless, it can be replaced in a few seconds by an interchangeable spare set of cones carried in the engine tool box. The central steam jet is . . . annular, with an air passage through its centre, which is used for either the induction of heated air or for the exhaustion of the automatic brake pipes on the train. An improved construction of the ring blower . . . [provided] six [steam] jets, two being drilled at varying angles to the centre line and placed immediately above and below the nozzle, whilst the remaining four are drilled parallel at equal distances from the centre—a combination which gives the maximum atomizing, distributing and air-inducing properties, with the minimum expenditure of steam, for whilst the angular jets distribute the fuel and flame the parallel ones induce air and ensure its absorption in the oil spray for securing good combustion."

The admission or cutting off of steam and oil fuel in the burners was controlled from the footplate by the fireman—a much less onerous duty than continually shovelling coal—the appropriate valves and cocks being easily operated by hand. Alertness was needed, since the demand for steam might be suddenly increased or reduced, which necessitated an immediate adjustment of the oil supply. One advantage of using oil fuel was that the fire did not invariably become 'dirty', clogged up with unburnt residues from the coal, as was commonly the case in a conventionally fired locomotive. In an oil-fired engine *all* the oil fuel burned in the firebox, so the firebed remained in much the same condition throughout the run.

Finished in the GER livery of royal blue lined out in black and red, and attached to tenders which looked sleeker than others from the absence of piled-up coal, these locomotives vied with their 4-2-2 sisters on the other lines for splendour of appearance, though their performances on a road with so many awkward gradients could never be as startling; working to generous schedules such as 88 minutes for the $68\frac{3}{4}$ miles from Liverpool Street to Ipswich, they did not need to be. They were employed for a mere two years on main line

express duties and were then replaced by the 4-4-0 'Claud Hamiltons', the first of which came out in 1900. They then followed their predecessors, the 2-2-2s, to the flatter lines of the Fenland and Lincolnshire.

* * *

During their brief two-year span on the principal main line trains they ran well, and impressed Rous-Marten, who devoted an article to them in *The Engineer* of 2nd December 1898, when he included a description of a journey made behind No. 19 on the principal Cromer express from Liverpool Street, and added a log which the author has shortened and, in places, ventured to amend.[1]
"On the occasion of my trip the load was the normal one, of 175 tons. The weather was fine and the rails dry. The Bethnal Green bank of 1 in 70 was ascended very easily, but near Coburn Road adverse signals brought us almost to a dead stand. Five miles further on heavy road repairs brought us down to 10 miles an hour for nearly a mile.[2] The steep bank past Brentwood was climbed very steadily, the minimum speed up the 1 in 84 being 25.7 miles an hour. The subsequent descent to Chelmsford was run mostly at 65.4 to 69.2 miles an hour and the short rise at 1 in 123 which follows was ascended at a minimum rate of 52.8. Another relaying slack was encountered soon after Kelvedon.

In spite of all hindrances Colchester was passed in 63 min 49 sec from the start. Water was picked up at speed just before passing Ipswich. The time to Ipswich was 81 min 59 sec, or 3 min 1 sec under booked time. Yet one more slack for relaying occurred, in this case near Diss, speed being reduced for a considerable distance. Soon afterward the maximum speed of this trip was attained, 70 miles an hour being just touched. Water was again picked up at speed near Tivetshall. Trowse station, 114 miles, was passed in 134 min 18 sec from London, but 7 min 14 sec had been lost by the various delays, so that the actual net time to Trowse for computing locomotive work was 127 min 4 sec.

1. Amendment was necessary because some of the published passing times were clearly inaccurate. Rous-Marten's statement that Colchester was passed in 62 min 49 sec from Liverpool Street is clearly wrong; it could not have travelled from Marks Tey to that station in a second under four minutes, which would have involved an average speed of over 72 mph, when he himself says later that 70 mph was the highest speed reached anywhere on the journey.
2. The passing times at Ilford and Chadwell Heath suggest that the reduction was not nearly so great—perhaps to 30 mph.

GER 4-2-2 No. 19,
Liverpool St–North Walsham

Miles		Min	Sec	Speeds (mph)
00.0	Liverpool Street	00	00	
	sigs			
04.0	Stratford	08	37	
07.3	Ilford	12	59	
	pws			
10.0	Chadwell Heath	17	14	
12.2	Romford	20	32	
15.1	Harold Wood	23	49	
18.2	Brentwood	28	15	Min beyond:
20.2	Shenfield	31	48	$25\frac{3}{4}$
23.5	Ingatestone	35	21	Max beyond:
29.8	Chelmsford	41	06	$69\frac{1}{4}$
35.9	Hatfield Peverel	47	42	
38.6	Witham	50	30	
42.2	Kelvedon	54	09	
	pws			
46.6	Marks Tey	58	50	
51.6	Colchester	63	49	
56.0	Ardleigh	68	35	
59.3	Manningtree	72	07	
63.1	Bentley	75	52	
68.7	Ipswich	81	59	
73.5	Claydon	87	30	
77.1	Needham	91	31	
80.8	Stowmarket	95	29	
83.0	Haughley	98	17	
86.6	Finningham	103	40	
91.3	Mellis	108	41	
	pws			
95.1	Diss	114	32	Max beyond:
100.6	Tivetshall	120	12	70
104.1	Forncett	124	00	
109.9	Swainsthorpe	129	28	
	service slack			
113.9	Trowse	134	18	
	service slack			
123.0	Salhouse	145	02	
126.0	Wroxham	148	06	Slack to pick up tablet for single line
130.5	North Walsham	158	39	

The remainder of the journey calls for little remark. The mile of 1 in 80 [2 miles past Trowse] was run at 36 miles an hour, and North Walsham, $130\frac{1}{2}$ miles, was reached in 2 hrs 38 min 58 sec—or in 2 hrs 31 min 44 sec net time from London. Our arrival at Cromer was punctual to the minute. The engine appeared to steam very freely and well throughout, and quicker time could easily have been made had this been desired. But absolute punctuality was observed and no more was needful."

E. L. Ahrons also wrote approvingly of these engines and noted the interest taken in them by their crews and the care bestowed on them. In the article cited earlier in this chapter he notes that:
"Both Norwich and Ipswich sheds did uncommonly good work with these [Cromer] expresses, not only as regards really excellent timekeeping, but also in immunity from engine failures, which were exceedingly rare. And it reflected much credit on all concerned—both officials and men. The engines were watched after the manner of mice by cats, and the very slightest sign of anything likely to go wrong was discovered and remedied at once."

He mentions a run on the 4.55 pm restaurant car express from Liverpool Street, when No. 19 with the (for its time) heavy load of 250 tons, lost $1\frac{1}{2}$ minutes to Shenfield, but had made up $1\frac{1}{4}$ minutes of this by Chelmsford, was 1 minute early at Colchester and $1\frac{1}{4}$ minutes early at Ipswich, reached in $86\frac{3}{4}$ minutes.

At the end of 1900 these locomotives were one by one taken off the principal main line expresses and put to work on the Great Northern & Great Eastern Joint Line between March and Doncaster, where they often worked through as far as York. The first to be withdrawn disappeared in 1907 after an active existence of only nine years, and the last vanished three years later. Before they were scrapped some had their oil burners removed and had tenders adapted for the use of coal alone, as one of the illustrations shows.

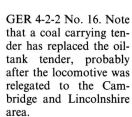
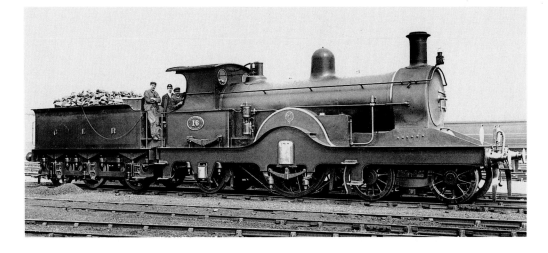

GER 4-2-2 No. 16. Note that a coal carrying tender has replaced the oil-tank tender, probably after the locomotive was relegated to the Cambridge and Lincolnshire area.
(*W. J. Barker Collection, NRM*)

11 The Great Northern Experimental Dozen

Why H. A. Ivatt, Patrick Stirling's successor as Locomotive Superintendent on the Great Northern Railway, should have built any single wheelers at all, is something of a puzzle. He had never built any for the Great Southern & Western of Ireland when he was in charge at Inchicore during his tenure of the superintendency there, and after taking office at Doncaster in 1895 he began at once to build coupled engines, first 4-4-0s, then 4-4-2s, for express passenger work, both of which designs, unlike those of Stirling's four-coupled engines, proved successful. According to his grandson, H. A. V. Bulleid, he "wanted convincing that there was no more to be had from the 'singles' so he designed and built a 4-2-2 with 7 ft 7½ in wheels, 18 in by 26 in cylinders, but larger boilers than Stirlings." Possibly he was affected by the prevailing sentiment in favour of the bogie single wheeler. More likely the last phrase in Bulleid's remark provides the clue.

Stirling's single wheelers were all under-boilered. They had coped, but towards the end only just, and needed great skill in driving. The GNR drivers had developed the necessary skills and had made Stirling's 2-2-2s and 4-2-2s perform almost impossibly well when put to it. But they had to run right up to the margin of their ability—and, furthermore, some of them were now nearly thirty years old. One could give them new boilers, as Ivatt did to some, but that was merely patching. If there were a use still for such engines, it would be better to build some designed around a larger boiler. One may conjecture that such were Ivatt's thoughts on the matter.

If there was indeed "more to be had from the singles" it would not be on the general run of the GNR's express trains but on certain lighter ones run to attract businessmen by giving a competitively fast service between King's Cross and Leeds or Sheffield. To the first-named city there were services on the Midland Railway already competing; to the second there were also MR services and, once the Great Central's London extension was in use, their trains would compete as well. To both places the GNR had the shortest and easiest route, and to retain its traffic it had to run services that were equally comfortable and noticeably faster. The answer seemed to lie in the provision of trains which were of up-to-date stock so that the businessman could comfortably do some work en route, but were very light and well within the capacity of the engines set to haul them. On such trains Stirling's single wheelers were being used, and for them Ivatt's new singles were designed.

W. A. Tuplin, in his book *Great Northern Steam*, suggests that the new engines were not really needed, and that the rebuilt Stirling singles would have done just as well. With the benefit of hindsight he may have been correct. Contemporary observers such as Charles Rous-Marten, however, were enthusiastic about the Ivatt singles, and the latter recorded a good many of their performances, for which the later historian is grateful.

Ivatt brought out the first of his 4-2-2s in October 1898, and then waited to see what it was like in practice before constructing any more. The engine had a massive appearance, since the boiler was pitched much higher than on any of Stirling's engines, or indeed on Ivatt's earliest 4-4-0s, with a centre-line 8 ft 3 in above the rails; the diameter, too, exceeded that of any which Stirling had built. The firebox, also, was larger, and the grate area was a quarter as much again. On the other hand, the cylinders were smaller than those of the 8-footers, having a shorter stroke. Ivatt was a great believer in having adequately sized boilers. His later large 4-4-2s, indeed, had boilers that were more than adequate, since they provided steam for cylinders that were smaller than those of his single wheelers.

The frames of the new engines were massive, extending well in front of the smokebox and curving laterally outwards at the rear to provide outside bearings for the axle of the trailing wheels. The sandboxes in front of the driving wheels were hidden behind a footstep which, unusually, had only one step instead of the more conventional two. The cab was of the standard Ivatt type, a modification of the Stirling type with the flat-topped roof extended backwards. The safety valves were beneath a small cover; Stirling's brass cone with curved sides now disappeared from the GNR.

* * *

Once the prototype, No. 266, had emerged from Doncaster Works it naturally attracted a good deal of interest, and Rous-Marten made two test journeys behind it to see what it could do, each on the 1.30 pm Leeds express from King's Cross, which he boarded at Peterborough and timed as far as Doncaster, the schedule being 92 minutes for the 79.6 miles. The load was 205 tons.

"Starting from Peterborough, No. 266 got away very smoothly and soon gathered speed, and was going at 60 miles per hour before the first five miles had been covered. When Essendine was passed the speed had not fallen below 56 miles per hour; at Bytham it was still 53, at Corby 50 and up the final length at 1 in 178 to Stoke Box the minimum was 45. The last 15¼ miles to the summit were run in 17 min 53 sec. The Grantham signals were adverse, so our speed had to be slowed to 10 miles per hour; nevertheless we passed Grantham station in 35 min 56 sec from the Peterborough start. Newark, 14½ miles, was passed in 14 min 1 sec from Grantham, although owing to adverse signals each station was passed at 10 miles an hour. Along the 7 miles of dead level past Carlton the engine steadily maintained 65 miles per hour, and up the following ascent, at 1 in 200 to Askham, the lowest speed was 51.7 miles an hour.

Approaching Retford a third signal check was encountered, once more bringing down the speed to 10 miles an hour, but nevertheless Retford was passed in 35 min 38 sec from Grantham, 33¼ miles, notwithstanding more than 4 minutes' delay which left the net time 31½ minutes. From Retford to the final stop at Doncaster the locomotive work was very remarkable. The three mile climb at 1 in 198 to Pipers Wood is twice broken by short level bits. Nevertheless, and although the ascent was started at 70 miles an hour, it was an extraordinarily smart performance to reach the top without the speed once dropping below 61.6 miles per hour. So swiftly did No. 266 slip along with the 205-ton load that the stop at Doncaster was made only 16 min 44 sec after Retford was passed, dead slow, the distance being 17½ miles. This is quite an exceptional achievement.

The complete run from Peterborough to Doncaster was done in 88 min 18 sec, including all delays. The net time was 82¼ minutes. the 50½ miles from Grantham to Doncaster occupied only 52 min 22 sec. This is the finest performance I have ever recorded over that length of line, when the road and the delays are taken into due account.''

GNR Ivatt 4-2-2s: Prototype No. 266 and Nos 92, 100, 261–265 and 267–270

	No. 266	Others
Boiler – length:	11 ft 4 in	11 ft 4 in
diameter:	4 ft 5 in	4 ft 5 in
Firebox – length:	7 ft	7 ft
Heating surface (sq ft) –		
firetubes:	1,143.8	1,143.8
firebox surface:	125.8	125.8
total:	1,269.6	1,269.6
Grate area:	23.2 sq ft	23.2 sq ft
Boiler pressure (lbs/sq in):	170	175
Cylinders:	18 in × 26 in	19 in × 26 in
Wheels – bogie:	3 ft 7½ in	3 ft 8 in
driving:	7 ft 7½ in	7 ft 8 in
trailing:	4 ft 1½ in	4 ft 2 in
Total wheelbase:	23 ft 0½ in.	23 ft 0½ in
Weight in working order:	47 tons 10 cwt	48 tons
Adhesion weight:	18 tons	18 tons
Tractive effort (at 85%		
of boiler pressure):	13,303 lbs	15,175 lbs

The second run on the same train, with a slightly heavier load and with a strong side wind, was possibly of equal merit; this time no speeds were recorded, but Grantham was passed in 36½ minutes, Newark in 50¼ minutes and Retford in 69 min 50 sec; the engine was then eased as it was before time and Doncaster was reached in 87 min 22 sec, or 83¼ minutes net. However, it was a short journey between Grantham and Peterborough a little later which most impressed Rous-Marten.

"[No. 266] took the Leeds dining car train, weighing 257 tons, from Grantham to Peterborough, 29¼ miles, start to stop, in 28 min 57 sec, the best performance over that stage I have ever noticed. Starting from Grantham, the new single wheeler vigorously attacked the 5½ miles unbroken rise at 1 in 200 and climbed it in 9 min 3 sec. This appeared to me an extraordinary performance for an engine having only 92.5 lbs of tractive force for every pound of effective steam pressure in the cylinders, hauling a load of 257 tons behind the tender. The subsequent descent towards Peterborough was very swiftly made, but could have been done even faster had not the driver been specially cautioned against excessive speed down the bank. As it was he maintained a nearly uniform high velocity along the level length approaching Peterborough and made a quick stop on reaching that station. The distance of 23¾ miles from Stoke Summit to the Peterborough stop were covered in 19 min 54 sec. These three experiences unquestionably stamp Mr Ivatt's new single wheeler as one of the most efficient express engines in the kingdom, even with heavy loads, upon gradients of moderate steepness.''

Performances such as these encouraged Ivatt to build a further eleven similar engines, somewhat modifying the design. All the wheels were given slightly thicker tyres, which increased the diameters of the driving wheels to 7 ft 8 in. Cylinder diameters were also increased by an inch, and the boiler pressure was raised by 5 lbs per square inch. The frames were also deepened, as can be seen most clearly beneath the smokebox when one compares a picture of the prototype with that of a later engine of the class. The slide valves were placed beneath the cylinders instead of to their sides, and were worked by rocking shafts from the valve gear. In the GNR livery of apple green lined out in red and black, these engines look handsome in an unemphatic sort of way. Each carried an oval brass plate in the centre of each splasher bearing the company's name, the works number and the date of construction.

Soon after the building of these 'Mark II' models, Rous-Marten made a number of journeys behind some of them and recorded them approvingly in the columns of *The Railway Magazine*; two are worth a mention here. The first occurred in July 1903, when No. 261 was set the task of hauling a 250-ton load from King's Cross to Doncaster on the newly accelerated 9.45 am Leeds express. The start was inauspicious, as the locomotive slipped badly on the 1 in 105 out of the terminus, and had scarcely got moving again when a severe permanent way slack at Finsbury Park brought the speed down once more. The climb to Potters Bar, therefore, was slow, no higher speed being reached up the 1 in 200 than 38¾ mph. Not until Hitchin was passed did the engine really get going. No speeds are given for the racing stretch between that station and Huntingdon, but a comparison of the times on this and the following run (where some speeds *are* given) suggests that a maximum well into the 80s was reached near Three Counties. Before and after Peterborough there were severe permanent way slowings which hampered the climb to Stoke Summit, where the minimum was just over 39 mph, and the train was late past Grantham, but energetic running from there to Retford and a minimum of 55¾ over the Pipers Wood hump sufficed to bring the train into Doncaster ¾ minute early in 165 minutes net time.

A couple of years later, on the "Sheffield and Manchester Flyer", No. 100, with a featherweight load

Above: GNR Ivatt experimental prototype 4-2-2 No. 266, built in 1898, compared with No. 267, built in 1900, the first of No. 266's successors. Note the much deeper framing below the smokebox. (*NRM*)

Left: GNR Ivatt 4-2-2 No. 263, at the head of a local train, probably in Lincolnshire. (*Tripp Collection, NRM*)

of only three 12-wheelers, which Rous-Marten estimated at 120 tons, a much faster run was achieved. Potters Bar was passed in 15 min 56 sec, with a minimum of $52\frac{1}{2}$ mph at the top of the 1 in 200; speed then rose rapidly to $80\frac{1}{2}$ at Hatfield and again to the same figure beyond Hitchin. A rate of $73\frac{3}{4}$ was maintained on the level past Tempsford, the 1 in 200 beyond Huntingdon was surmounted at 56 and $77\frac{1}{2}$ was reached beyond. Signals at Peterborough slowed the train almost to a halt, but speed rapidly picked up on the level to $66\frac{1}{4}$ beyond Tallington, dropped to 60 at Little Bytham and eventually fell to 45 at Stoke. A faster climb could no doubt have been made but the train was now before time. There were no fireworks beyond Grantham, but 70 was maintained on the level beyond the crossing of the Trent and the minimum at Askham Summit was just 60. Retford was passed in $139\frac{1}{4}$ minutes in only a little over even time from London and more than ten minutes faster than on the previous run. The curve to the Sheffield branch, one of the sharpest in the country, was negotiated with extreme caution, and the 23 largely uphill miles to Sheffield were done in under 30 minutes; the latter was reached a minute early. This run demonstrated how easily these locomotives could cope on the fast, lightly loaded services for which they were designed. Both runs are tabulated herewith from the scanty detail provided by Rous-Marten.

Ivatt singles, King's Cross–Doncaster/Sheffield

Locomotive:		No. 261		No. 100		
Load:		250 tons		120 tons		
Miles		Min	Sec	Min	Sec	Speed
00.0	King's Cross	00	00	00	00	
		pws				
12.7	Potters Bar	19	42	15	56	$52\frac{1}{2}$
17.7	Hatfield	25	13	20	34	$80\frac{1}{2}$
22.0	Welwyn	29	14			
31.9	Hitchin	39	01	33	12	
36.9	Arlesey	42	53			$80\frac{1}{2}/73\frac{3}{4}$
58.9	Huntingdon	62	30	56	45	
						$56/77\frac{1}{2}$
				sigs		
76.4	Peterborough	79	39	74	14	
		pws (2)				$66\frac{1}{4}/60/45$
105.5	Grantham	116	00	106	24	
						70/60
120.1	Newark	129	49			
138.6	Retford	149	32	139	13	Severe slowing
156.0	Doncaster	167	11			
162.8	Sheffield			169	03	

W. A. Tuplin seems not to have thought much of these locomotives. In his book *Great Northern Steam* he gives his opinion that, "with adhesion weight restricted to 18 tons they were no better in getting away from rest [than the Stirling singles]. There is in fact no evidence that the Ivatt singles beat the best Stirling singles in any way."

He does not seem, however, to have done his homework. Cecil J. Allen, who timed some of these engines during their last days, published in the April 1914 *Railway Magazine* a number of runs on the 7.31 pm from Grantham to York, timed to passing Doncaster; the locomotives concerned included one of Stirling's last and largest 8-footers and two of Ivatt's 7 ft 8 in singles. A comparison of the performances of these engines suggests that the Ivatt 4-2-2s *could* get away rapidly from rest and *did* in fact beat the Stirling 8-footers, in one case despite having a load two coaches heavier. In Allen's words:

"A very slow start was made by No. 1008, as might be expected with driving wheels of so large a diameter, but some fine running followed, such times as 13 min 25 sec for the 15 miles from Hougham to Carlton and 8 min 40 sec for the $9\frac{1}{4}$ level miles from Retford to Bawtry indicating really fine work on the part of the engine. Doncaster would have been passed in 54 min but for a bad permanent way check beyond Rossington.

I have always found Mr Ivatt's handsome bogie singles of the 266 class capable of excellent work, and runs 3 and 4 are no exception to the rule, the first, with a load of 200 tons, being positively brilliant. For a single driver the start was astonishing ... Speed averaged 72 miles an hour from Hougham to Carlton, where 'even time' had been improved on, but thenceforward the running was easier in character, particularly from Markham Summit to Retford, where a pronounced slack was made. Otherwise we should probably have passed Doncaster in less than 51 min, but as it was a fine ascent to Pipers Wood took us from Bawtry to Doncaster in the fast time of $8\frac{3}{4}$ minutes, and through the latter town in $51\frac{3}{4}$ minutes.

Comparative, Stirling and Ivatt singles

Run No:			3		4	
Locomotive:		1008		266		268
Load (tons):		200		200		260
Miles		Min	Sec	Min	Sec	Min	Sec
---	---	---	---	---	---	---	---
00.0	Grantham	00	00	00	00	00	00
06.0	Hougham	09	50	08	20	10	05
14.6	Newark	17	15	15	20	16	15
20.9	Carlton	23	15	20	50	21	50
26.4	Tuxford	29	10	26	20	27	55
33.1	Retford	36	25	33	50	35	35
38.4	Ranskill	41	50	39	15	41	15
42.2	Bawtry	45	05	43	00	44	55
		pws					
50.5	Doncaster	56	50	51	45	53	40

Run No. 4 is more recent, and shows the work of this class with a heavier load. The same characteristics are again apparent—a fast start to Carlton, a moderate time from Tuxford to Retford, and excellent work over Pipers Wood Summit. It is a matter of no little regret to me that of recent years these engines have been taken off this train.

I have a large number of timings made behind them and have found them quite the most consistent time-keepers on the Great Northern Railway when reasonably loaded. As far as load goes, moreover, I have it on reliable authority that an engine of this type has kept time on this train—94 min from Grantham to York—with no less than 52 axles behind the tender.''

However, GNR single wheelers, whether Stirling's or Ivatt's, were by the time Allen wrote considered as yesterday's engines. The First World War was about to erupt, and before the signing of the Armistice in 1918 all the Ivatt singles had become scrap metal. H. N. Gresley, who succeeded to the GNR locomotive superintendency in 1911, decided that they were of no use and took the whole dozen out of service in one fell swoop. The accompanying photograph shows them standing in a melancholy line outside Doncaster Works, the one nearest to the camera being already in course of dismemberment.

GNR No. 265, built in 1901, on a King's Cross–Grimsby train at Boston, Lincs. (*Pilcher Collection, NRM*)

All twelve GNR Ivatt 4-2-2s awaiting scrapping at Doncaster late in 1918. The nearest one is already being dismantled.

(*NRM*)

12 The Great Central's Unwanted Half-Dozen

The final year of the 19th century saw the emergence from Gorton Works of the last type of single wheeler to be designed and built for a British line, and which almost as soon as it appeared was considered surplus to requirements. When the Board of the Manchester, Sheffield & Lincolnshire Railway decided towards the end of that century to take the immense financial risk of building an extension to London—a step which never financially justified itself, though railway enthusiasts may be glad of it since it added a few more deities to the gods in their Pantheon—it was necessary to construct new locomotives to work upon it.

The intention was to capture traffic from other lines which linked Sheffield, Nottingham and Leicester with London and (by way of the Great Western) also to tap West-to-North traffic through a branch from Woodford on the new line to London which diverged to link with the GWR's line from Oxford to Birmingham at Banbury. On the London services it was intended to provide light but well-appointed expresses which would match the existing services of the Midland and GNR, and lure would-be travellers by superior comfort and such inducements as buffet services. So the first thoughts of the locomotive department, and the last thoughts of its Locomotive Superintendent, Mr H. Pollitt, before his translation to a higher post, were directed towards the design of a suitable single wheeler. Pollitt specified that ten should be built. However, his successor, J. G. Robinson, had assumed office before the first of these new engines was completed, and he, like Churchward on the GWR, was a coupled-wheels man. He cancelled the last four in the order allowing only six to be produced.

Pollitt's design was really a variant of the 4-4-0s he was building at Gorton at about the same time, with trailing wheels beneath the cab instead of rear coupled wheels, and single driving wheels which were of a 7 ft 9 in diameter. It turned out to be a good-looking engine despite its chimney which may be described as a tidied-up stove-pipe. Like its contemporaries on the GNR it had inside frames; unlike them and any other single wheelers so far built it had a Belpaire firebox. The GCR never used any other type of firebox on any of its express locomotives—again, as on the GWR under Churchward.

This type had certain advantages over the round-topped firebox. For one thing, it allowed more space for water contact round the firebox sides. For another, it was easier, between flat surfaces, to stay the top of the inner firebox to the top of the outer firebox. If it had a disadvantage it was in restricting slightly the line of sight along the boiler sides from the spectacle windows in the cab, but since so many locomotive engineers were now going over to its use this cannot have been a serious drawback.

The Pollitt single wheeler had large cylinders, as large as those fitted to the latest MR 'Spinners', and piston valves instead of slide valves. When first built its boiler pressure was no less than 200 lbs per square inch; no other single wheeler matched it in this respect. The plate springs supporting the bogie and trailing wheels and the coil springs on the driving wheel axle were out of sight, though the latter could be seen through the wheel spokes. There were a few odd features. Whereas the cab roof of a steam locomotive usually extended an inch or two over the spectacle plate, in these engines it was the latter which extended slightly upwards above the level of the roof. The safety valves over the firebox were unusually tall, projecting prominently from a bulging protrusion like the base of a sawn-off dome. Two whistles were provided.

Those engines which carried a Pollitt chimney were distinctive though not unsightly, the latter's upper edge being thickened into a lip, and the base curving back to the outer surface of the smokebox. Some of the six were, however, given Robinson's more graceful design of chimney from the start, and all eventually came to possess one. The driving wheels were supplied with sand by steam blast from front and rear; the rear sandbox was prominent beneath the running plate just behind the driving wheel splasher, while the front one was less visible as a flat-topped box to the rear of the footstep. The tender had no side rails or side plates to allow the piling up of coal—rather surprising when runs of up to 164 miles were expected to be done with only the briefest of station stops.

In the Great Central livery adopted when the London Extension was built these engines looked a splendid sight. Boiler, dome, firebox, cab sides, tenders and wheel splashers were in Brunswick green, as were the wheels. The running boards, and those parts of the main frame which supported the smokebox, the footsteps, sandboxes and buffers were in crimson lake, and the whole was picked out in white and black. The company's coat of arms adorned the centre of each splasher. There were some variations in the manner of attaching the numbers to the cab sides; in two they were painted on while the rest had similarly positioned brass plates, two rectangular and two elliptical.

In his book *Great Central Steam*, W. A. Tuplin has some interesting remarks to make about these locomotives:

"The Pollitt singles were intended for the London extension with the knowledge that the trains would not be heavy on that route for some years ahead, and that 4-2-2s were handling many of the heaviest trains on the adjoining Midland main line. It is true that a single with 18 tons on the driving axle was adequate for a four-coach train of about 120 tons on gradients as steep as 1 in 100 in normal circumstances, but it is the abnormal circumstance that causes trouble. Imagine for example a southbound single with a load heavier than usual stopped by signal at Wendover on a 1 in 117 up grade on a slippery day when the steam sanding gear had frozen up. All the conditions are unusual, but that is no guarantee against their occurring at the same time. If the combination did occur the single might take a very long time to get safely moving again . . .

GCR Pollitt 4-2-2
No. 971, with Robinson
chimney, built in Nov-
ember 1900.
(*Chisholm Collection,
NRM*)

Pollitt 4-2-2 No. 968
early in its career, heading a northbound ex-
press from Marylebone
on Metropolitan Rail-
way metals near North-
wood, the line having
not yet been electrified.
(*NRM*)

*Apart from such exceptional circumstances the Pollitt
singles may well have been ideal for the early Great
Central express trains ... With a grate area of 24.8 square
feet they had greater boiler power than all other British
singles and all Great Central 4-4-0s until 1913 and, unless
defective in some un-obvious way, had the power and speed
to make mile-a-minute averages with 120-ton trains. But
no very striking schedule was adopted in the first year or
two of the London extension as there was a need to
consolidate some of the embankments by traffic running at
moderate speeds, and by the time this restriction was lifted
enough locomotives of Robinson's first 4-4-0 design had
been built to handle the main line trains into Marylebone
and out of it."*

This is probably the reason why, although a number
of photographs exist to show these engines at work on
the London Extension—one appears here—there were
no records taken of their running on these trains because
of temporarily slowed schedules. The Pollitt singles, so

Above: Great Central Railway, Pollitt 4-2-2 No. 969, with original chimney, as built in August 1900.   (*NRM*)

Below: GCR No. 969 after being fitted with the larger Robinson boiler and an increased capacity tender.   (*NRM*)

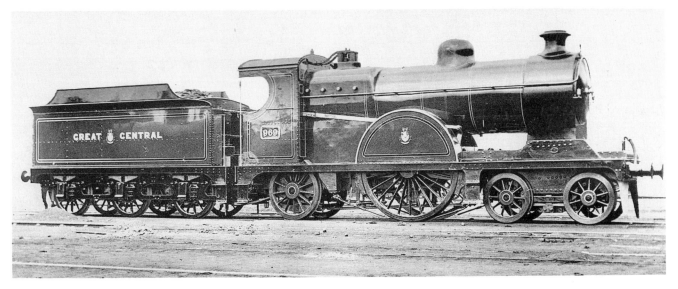

far as ability to perform went, were rather like the young woman in the Victorian song, who took her harp to the party but nobody asked her to play.

✳ ✳ ✳

The only indication the writer has been able to find relevant to their running on the London Extension is a small-print mention in *The Railway Magazine* for May 1901:

No. 967, one of the new single engines, took charge of the 7.44 pm train, consisting of five coaches, at Leicester, and travelled over the 11 miles 38 chains from Lutterworth to Willoughby in 10 min 19 sec, of which the 4 miles 55 chains from Rugby to Willoughby were passed over in 3 min 54 sec, or at a speed of about 73 mph. The 4 miles 63 chains

from Brackley to Finmere were negotiated in 4 min 22 sec. The 35 miles 43 chains from Lutterworth to Finmere were travelled over in 35 min 15 sec, so that the average speed for this distance exceeded 60 mph. The train arrived at Marylebone 2 min 17 sec before time.

If only the writer had taken the trouble to include a complete log instead of expanding his information to occupy as much space as possible, this tantalizing glimpse would have been more valuable.

Once the single wheelers had been displaced from the London Extension, work was found for them in the North Midlands and the North West, on the mainly level lines between Sheffield and Lincoln or Grimsby, and more importantly on the Cheshire Lines Committee's fast interval services between Manchester and Liverpool,

No. 969 as rebuilt a second time with the original type of boiler and also superheated—hence the extended smokebox—in LNER livery and re-numbered 5969.
(*Ken Nunn Collection, LCGB*)

some of which carried through carriages from the latter city to St Pancras. The Great Central shared with the MR the working of these trains.

Rous-Marten, in a *Railway Magazine* article in September 1904, describes briefly, a non-stop run from Liverpool to Manchester behind No. 967, with six vehicles weighing 180 tons, in which the 40-minute schedule for the 34.1 miles was cut to 35 min 54 sec, with no lower speed anywhere than 56 mph and a maximum of nearly 70. This line, unlike the lines in Lincolnshire, is by no means a level road, but saw-tooth in its inclinations. It includes $2\frac{1}{2}$ miles at 1 in 185 in both directions, down from Farnworth and up to Hunts Cross, and a few shorter but steeper pitches, especially on either side of the bridge crossing the Manchester Ship Canal and on the approach to Manchester Central from the west. The load, too, was rather heavier than these locomotives were expected to haul on the Marylebone line—though there the gradients were on the whole both longer and steeper. So these single wheelers were not exactly put out to grass, like the Stirling 8-footers in their old age.

Besides the change made by Robinson to their chimneys, some considerable rebuilding befell four of these engines later in their career. In 1911 No. 969 was given a new boiler, one of the kind currently being fitted to Robinson's 'Coronation' 4-6-2 tank engines, wider than the original boiler and pitched 7 inches higher; this necessitated the fitting of a new cab with a roof extending to the rear of the footplate and supported there by pillars. It did not last long in this form, but while it did it looked most impressive and deceptively powerful. In 1915 No. 969 was given its former type of boiler again, and a Robinson superheater, the smokebox being extended to take the latter; the following year No. 967 was similarly treated, as were Nos 970 and 972 in 1919. These four were the only single wheelers ever to receive superheat. One would very much like to know what kind of performances they subsequently achieved.

It should also be added that Robinson reduced the working pressure of these engines to a mere 160 lbs per

square inch after they were taken off the London Extension; 190 lbs was the most he ever gave any engine, and many of his smaller ones had only 160 lbs. He evidently thought the single wheelers did not need the high pressure they were first given for their subsequent easier duties and that it was preferable that their boilers should last longer.

These engines all lasted long enough to pass into LNER ownership. No. 971 was the first to be withdrawn, in December 1923; the last to go was No. 972 in August 1927. This locomotive, before its demise, had the distinction of taking part in the 1925 Stockton & Darlington Railway Centenary celebrations, steaming slowly in procession behind *Locomotion No. 1* and other worthies of the past.

GCR Pollitt 4-2-2s Nos 967–972

Boiler – length:	11 ft 2 in
diameter:	4 ft 3 in*
Firebox (Belpaire) – length:	8 ft**
Heating surface – firetubes:	957 sq ft
firebox surface:	132 sq ft
total:	1,089 sq ft***
Grate area:	24.8 sq ft
Boiler pressure:	200 lbs per sq in
Cylinders:	$19\frac{1}{2}$ in × 26 in
Wheels – bogie:	3 ft 6 in
driving:	7 ft 9 in
trailing:	4 ft 6 in
Total wheelbase:	22 ft 11 in
Weight in working order:	51 tons 3 cwt
Adhesion weight:	18 tons
Tractive effort (before lowering of boiler pressure):	18,072 lbs
Tractive effort (after lowering of boiler pressure to 160 psi):	14,457 lbs

*As finally rebuilt the diameter was 4 ft 9 in.
**As finally rebuilt it was 7 ft.
***For subsequently superheated engines the total was 1,043, including 138 sq ft superheating surface.

13 Assessment and Analysis

Looking back now at the final generation of single wheelers, the last of which was built over ninety years ago, is rather like surveying a distant period of history. The dust has settled over old enthusiasms and former disputes. Apart from a couple of preserved examples the engines themselves are no more; indeed, the steam locomotive itself, in these islands and most other parts of the world, has all but vanished into history. Writing about them is rather like writing about the English Civil War. One cannot take sides with Cavaliers or Roundheads as their contemporaries did, but they make an interesting imaginative spectacle and one's sympathies are still to some extent aroused. So it is with the bogie single wheelers—they have become 'such stuff as dreams are made of, and their little life is rounded with a sleep'.

The dispassionate railway historian (if there could be such a person!) may now attempt to pronounce his judgements, both on the locomotives themselves and on the whole enterprise of their production. Which was the most successful design, and which the least? As to the latter, perhaps the two Irish engines have to be so regarded. They were the first to come and the first to go; they were evidently not so successful as to warrant the construction of more, and they were soon taken off the trains they were designed to haul. But it is a pity that we know nothing of how they performed—how fast, for example, they ran down Adavoyle bank and whether they ever equalled the legendary feats of Glover's 4-4-0 No. 190 in the years between the wars, or of his blue-painted compounds.

As to which were the most successful, some (with the present writer) would say that Johnson's 'Spinners' deserved that distinction. They were kept in active service longer than any other 4-2-2s, albeit towards the end rather for piloting than for pulling, and one or two had 90 mph maxima recorded to their credit. Others may regard Dean's engines as the real stars, especially in view of *Duke of Connaught*'s achievement on 9th May 1904.

With their high boiler pressure and large grate area, Pollitt's singles, as originally built, had perhaps the greatest potential, and it is a thousand pities that they never had the opportunity to display themselves on the Great Central main line after its trackbed had consolidated sufficiently to allow fast running. And if the 'reliable source' which Cecil J. Allen mentioned is to be trusted, Ivatt's dozen had the ability to keep time with trains of 400 tons, something no single wheeler was surely ever asked to do on a 53 miles-an-hour schedule. So it is not easy to award the palm.

Had loads remained more or less at the 1890 level, one might perhaps have seen this type perpetuated and improved for the lighter services, and 4-4-0s for the heavier ones. Improved track would have permitted 20 tons or more to be placed on each pair of driving wheels, without this having to be done surreptitiously in the hope that the Civil Engineer would not find out. Larger boilers could no doubt have been fitted, as Churchward did to some of Dean's engines and Robinson to one of Pollitt's. Superheating would have been provided as a matter of course. Driving wheel diameters would have probably stabilized at about 7 feet. The additional grace of the single wheeler engine could have been exploited for publicity purposes.

But what was sauce for the two-wheeled goose was also sauce for the four-wheeled gander. All the improvements a single could receive could also be given to coupled engines, which could be made just as shapely and magnificent, as Wainwright was to show on the South Eastern & Chatham. Once it was found in practice that coupled wheels were no hindrance to free running, the advantages of having an engine that could be overloaded if necessary outweighed the extra wear and tear on the moving parts. *Duke of Connaught* shed glory on all his tribe when running the mails to Paddington from Bristol on that auspicious May morning, but *City of Truro* had already demonstrated that it could have done as well or better if asked to. Even Whale's 4-6-0 'Experiments' on the London & North Western showed themselves equal to 90 mph running. In the contest between the single wheeler and the coupled engine, while the former was given a timely boost by the discovery of the steam sand blast, the latter eventually overtook it.

The feelings of contemporaries regarding the single wheeler are mirrored in the pages of *The Railway Magazine* and more particularly in the articles on *Locomotive Practice & Performance* by Charles Rous-Marten. He was temperamentally attracted to the type, but found himself bound in the end to recognize that its day was done. From the commencement of his series of articles he made reference, over and over again, to single wheelers, commending their virtues and regretting their shortcomings. In July 1904 he devoted almost the whole of his article to a discussion of singles versus coupled engines, ranging widely over the different types of single wheeler and quoting some of their outstanding achievements. His conclusion seemed then to be that the single, because of the fewness of its moving parts, was the ideal type for using on fast, light trains.

"The question that arises out of that remarkable run by the Duke of Connaught is whether it will be found desirable to establish a separate class of extra-fast limited expresses, and to build a separate class of single wheelers on purpose to run them ... There will doubtless be plenty to argue that the policy of conveying passengers at a penny a mile by all trains is sacro-sanct (say as Free Trade itself!) and ought not to be departed from in any circumstances. But the point is this: the penny-a-milers would still enjoy every advantage they had before. They would travel as fast, as comfortably, as often, as punctually, even by the same trains. Only, a new class of 'special expresses', limited as to load and more expensive as to fares, would be run at other times than those now in force, for the benefit of such passengers as should choose to pay extra

for the sake of enhanced swiftness. It would be the case of the London, Brighton and South Coast Sunday Limited Pullman, or of that relief train which inaugurated the London and North Western Railway's 3½-hour service between London and Manchester. In the latter case, it will be remembered, a special train weighing 110 tons per engine left Euston at 10.32 and reached Manchester in 3 hours 26 minutes. The regular 10.35 am, itself booked at 55.2 miles an hour as far as Stafford, followed three minutes later ... and carried its crowd of passengers to Manchester and Liverpool in the usual way. Did any of these latter suffer from the favoured few being taken on in front of them? Surely not ... The plan is largely in operation in the two most democratic countries on earth—the great republics of France and America."

Several paragraphs follow in which the performances of *Duke of Connaught* and *City of Truro* are compared and analysed. His final judgement was:

"I simply record the plain facts and figures. They strongly support the view I have always held and expressed, that for such duty the single wheeler type is absolutely pre-eminent in suitability. But the question still remains whether it would be economically advantageous to maintain a special type for such special work, in view of the splendid speed records achieved by coupled engines, which latter can also haul trains far too heavy for any single wheeler. The question is one of practice, not of theory, and fortunately abundant means are now at hand of testing it thoroughly. [He then lists the existing types of singles on the English main lines.] All of these are very fine engines and might well be compared systematically as to results with the equally fine coupled engines possessed by each of the lines named."

The question of whether it might be desirable to run special high-speed trains—something which both the GWR and LNER set out to do in the years immediately preceding the Second World War, with great success—raises an interesting topic. Would it indeed have been a good idea to build single wheelers specially for such trains? To some extent this was already happening. The GNR, as already noticed in Chapter 11, had its fast expresses between London and Sheffield and Leeds, which were run with four or even three very opulent vehicles of the latest stock behind either Stirling 2-2-2s or Ivatt 4-2-2s. They were fast, but not quite in the "Cheltenham Flyer" or "Bristolian" bracket, let alone the "Silver Jubilee" and "Coronation". They were a little faster than existing trains but not a whole lot faster. Nor were they retained for very long. Round about mid-decade their timings were eased. The Great Central similarly put on a special fast train to Sheffield and Manchester, but that too did not long endure, and in any case was never meant to be worked by a single wheeler. However, these trains were not what Rous-Marten had in mind; he was thinking of extra fare, or perhaps 1st class-only trains.

There would probably not have been a great demand for them in the Edwardian period. Fewer businessmen travelled then than now—indeed, fewer members of the general public then used the railways for great distances. This is evident if one studies contemporary timetables. The affluence that permits frequent travel had not then spread very far down the social system. People stayed at home, going for occasional day outings, or for short seaside holidays at a watering place conveniently near. One did not visit one's distant relations frequently; one wrote them letters instead. The young did not wander all over the country as they do now over the whole globe. However, perhaps the experiment might have paid, to have put on a special businessmen's service from London to Birmingham and back at, say, 110 minutes each way, or a similar 3-hour service to Manchester. The LNWR might have tried it. But it would not have needed to use single wheelers, and it had no up-to-date ones on its system. It might have built half a dozen, but to what end? The trouble with a single wheeler was that it was not versatile. The economies that it might achieve in running would be marginal; the time it would have to spend standing idle would have been great.

Moreover, the vaunted advantage that the single enjoyed, of having fewer moving parts, was not so important, from the points of view of both speed and economy, as the freedom by which steam could be got into and out of the cylinders. Front end design is something that Rous-Marten never discusses, but even in his time its importance was beginning to be realized; Churchward, for example, was aware of it—hence the fact that not only *City of Truro*, but also *all* his coupled express engines could run freely. Had he attempted to run a specially fast Bristol service in 1905 he would probably have drafted 'Cities' for the work.

How then may one sum up the whole inside-cylindered bogie single phenomenon? As works of art they were superb, and if such things are entitled to exist independently of their practical value, like sculptures and paintings, one cannot regret that they were ever built, and one could wish that an example of each had been preserved. But steam locomotives are not built simply for people to look at. They were an act of faith on the part of designers who believed that the steam sand blast had given them the possibility of performing as well as coupled engines on the generality of express services, and they were preferred for their simplicity and the fact that they cost less to build. Up to about the middle of the 1890s they were a success, but then loads began to tell. The type continued where the possibility of lightly loaded expresses continued. But only two lines built large numbers, and only one line went on improving the breed. Fifteen years saw their rise and fall as newly constructed machines; 25 years saw the end of their employment on express passenger trains. They were beautiful creations and it was good that they appeared and flourished for a while. But their end, like the later end of the steam locomotive, was inevitable.

Bibliography

Ahrons, E. L. *Locomotive & Train Working in the Latter Part of the 19th Century: Vols 1-5* (Heffer & Co, 1951-4)
Ahrons, E. L. *The British Steam Railway Locomotive: 1825-1925* (Reprint) (Bracken Books, 1987)
Baxter, B., ed Baxter, D. *British Locomotive Catalogue: 1825-1923, Volumes 3, 4, 5A and 5B* (Moorland Pub Co, 1984)
Bradley, D. L. *The Drummond Greyhounds* (David & Charles, 1977)
Bulleid, H. A. V. *Master Builders of Steam* (Ian Allan, 1963)
Campbell-Cornwell, H. J. *William Stroudley, Craftsman of Steam* (David & Charles, 1968)
Campbell-Cornwell, H. J. *Forty years of Caledonian Locomotives* (David & Charles, 1974)
Haresnape, B. & Rowledge, P. *Drummond Locomotives* (Ian Allan, 1982)
Haresnape, B. & Rowledge, P. *Robinson Locomotives* (Ian Allan, 1982)
Haresnape, B. *Stroudley Locomotives* (Ian Allan, 1985)
Hoole K. *An Illustrated History of N.E.R. Locomotives* (OPC, 1988)
Leech, K. H. & Boddy, M. G. *The Stirling Singles* (David & Charles 1965)
Nock, O. S. *Locomotives of the North Eastern Railway* (Ian Allan, 1954)
Nock, O. S. *Speed Records on British Railways* (David & Charles, 1971)
Rolt, L. T. C. *Patrick Stirling's Locomotives* (Hamish Hamilton, 1964)
Tuplin, W. A. *Great Central Steam* (Allen & Unwin, 1967)
Tuplin, W. A. *North Eastern Steam* (Allen & Unwin, 1970)
Tuplin, W. A. *Great Northern Steam* (Ian Allan, 1971)
Tuplin, W. A. *Midland Steam* (David & Charles, 1973)

Several articles in *The Engineer* and *The Railway Magazine* were also consulted.

Index